Pipe Bomb for the Soul

Alice Bag

Introduction

One morning, driving home from one of my punk rock all-nighters, I stopped at a traffic light and through my car window I could see 1980 off in the horizon. It was approaching like a fast train and I got the feeling that I either had to jump on the train or get run over by it, so I jumped.

By the fall of 1979, I was back at college with the intention of becoming a lawyer. I studied, worked, and played music, and in 1984, I graduated from Cal State Los Angeles with a degree in Philosophy. I was still thinking of law school while working part time as a teacher's aid to scrounge up a little cash. It wasn't my plan to fall in love with teaching, but that's how love is. It sneaks up on you. Those kids were like Visine for tired eyes, they started each day eager to be surprised by what was in store for them. Nothing beats the moment when a child discovers the answer to a puzzle, when numbers, or letters, or shapes make sense. The joy that radiates from them warms you. I wanted to bask in that everyday.

I took a couple of tests, signed up for an accelerated teaching program at USC, applied for an emergency bilingual teaching credential, and started teaching at Hoover Street Elementary. My students were Spanish-speaking kids from Mexico and Central America. Some were born in the U.S., others were immigrants. They reminded me of myself. I'd started school not knowing any English and the road to English fluency had been a bumpy one. Now I was in a position to make their journey a little smoother. I knew that there was a high dropout rate for kids who grew up like me, kids for whom day to day survival could be more important than anything in a textbook. I wanted to challenge those statistics. I was a fighter, I thought I could fight for them.

It took less than a year before my student debt at USC led me back to Cal State L.A. There, I met a wise philosophy professor who tried to show me new ways of learning. His name was Dr. Vick. Around the same time, another professor assigned Pedagogy of the Oppressed by Paulo Freire as part of the required reading list. It was a one-two punch. In his writing, Freire describes the kind of education I had been exposed to as a child, one that either alienates the students completely or indoctrinates them with values that support the status quo. He denounces a system that creates a one-way flow of ideas, without ever teaching children to evaluate information through the use of higher level thinking skills or to contribute their own ideas. I started wondering how I could improve the quality of education I was giving my students, but my thoughts were rudely interrupted.

The devastating Mexico City quake of 1985

In September of 1985, a magnitude 8.5 earthquake struck Mexico City. It shook me to the core. I had family there, and though they they hadn't been injured, every Mexican and person of Mexican heritage felt the aftershocks. I wanted to help, so I did the only thing that popped into my head. I called my musician friends and tried to organize a benefit concert to raise money for the Red Cross relief efforts. The only problem was that I had never put together a concert, and I soon discovered that it was a monumental task. I threw all my energy into coordinating the event, all the while ignoring and irritating my long-time boyfriend, Bruce.

We raised very little money and after it was all over I felt completely drained and demoralized. I had wasted so much energy and accomplished so little. I wanted badly to make a difference but I had no experience doing this type of event. I felt impotent but even as I sat on my bed in a dark, gloomy mood, the stubborn, resilient side of me sparked a flash of rebellion against the self pity I was feeling. I could make a difference, I thought, if I just tried a little harder. Organizing the benefit concert had put pressure on an already strained relationship. Bruce seemed to be in his own world. He showed little interest in what had been a very important project for me. It just felt like another aftershock when he and I decided to take a break after having been together for 7 years. I briefly dated the club owner who had helped me organize the concert but romance wasn't what I was looking for at that point in my life. I craved involvement in the world around me.

Back at school, my friend Kathy and I sipped coffee between classes and discussed Paulo Freire. We were in agreement with his view that education is used by the dominant elite culture to deposit ideas into the minds of students, a practice he calls the Banking Method. We were all too familiar with it. We knew that some teachers made you feel like a troublemaker if you questioned authority and that a big part of making it through school depended on regurgitating facts or parroting the views of the lecturer. We didn't want to be receptacles, filled with the values of the dominant class, and we certainly didn't want to turn our students into that. We wanted our students to talk back, to have their own points of view and be able to express them. We wanted our students to shape the world, not be herded through it.

Kathy mentioned that Paulo Freire had been involved in helping the post-revolutionary government of Nicaragua with their literacy campaign. I was fascinated, not only because of Freire, but because many of my students were from Central America, and the Sandinista revolution was like a live Petri dish. It seemed that the whole world was watching to see if the Sandinistas would succeed. A few days later, Kathy gave me a small pamphlet for a place called The Nica School, where one could volunteer to work in Nicaragua, learn about the revolution, and live with a local family. There was an option to learn Spanish through immersion, but my first language is Spanish, so I knew that part of the program wasn't for me.

I told my parents I was thinking of going to Nicaragua. They insisted that I shouldn't go, reminding me that the country was at war and that Nicaragua was being described as the "new Cuba." I wholeheartedly supported the Sandinista movement which had successfully overthrown the corrupt government of Anastasio Somoza and installed a socialist democracy in its place, but instead, I focused on the education angle with my parents. "This is going to help me be a better teacher, plus, I'll get college credit!" As I was trying to soothe their nerves, the nightly television news began showing a clip of tanks rolling through the capital city of Managua. "See? That's where you want to go!" my father yelled at the screen, visibly concerned.

"Don't worry, the town where I'm going is far away from Managua. I'll be safe," I said. "I'm not going to join the revolution." Little did I know that much of the fighting was taking place in the northern part of the country where I'd be living and that the very act of teaching someone to read could be revolutionary.

Now, the only thing left to do was to figure out how I could make good on the claim that I would get college credit for the journey. I pitched the idea of going to Nicaragua to study their educational reforms to Professor Vick. I proposed an independent study for college credit. I'm not sure that he was as interested in the report I was required to write as he was about the possibility of me stepping outside of my intellectual rut. Dr. Vick wisely made his approval contingent upon what seemed like an unusual requirement: that I keep a journal of my time in Nicaragua, not to turn in, but to help me understand my journey.

This book is based on that journal.

I use the following icons in the book.
Here's what they mean.

Fuck This!
Wrong thinking, bad ideas.

Seeds for Germination: Ideas that penetrated my subconscious and later had an impact on my life.

Upon Reflection: Seeing my actions from a distance has helped me gain a clearer understanding of what was happening in different situations.

Fun Size History: A quick overview meant to aid in the understanding of the diary.

3/30/86, Sunday

The flight boarded late but we're finally on the plane. At last on my way to Nicaragua! I'm so excited that even though almost everyone on the plane is sleeping I can't keep my eyelids shut. It's almost 1:00 am and I'm really tired but I can't settle down.

A few minutes ago I put my head back and closed my eyes trying to relax and doze but I heard the two men behind me talking. I know it's rude to listen but their conversation drew me in. I heard an inquisitive traveler ask his neighbor where he was heading.

"I'm catching a connecting flight down to Central America," the neighbor replied.

I too was catching a connecting flight to Central America, so his response piqued my interest. I was tempted to turn around and make friends with him right away. Maybe he was going to the Nica school, too!

Thank god for the little bit of impulse control that kept me from doing that. The inquisitive traveler continued asking questions.

"What takes you to Central America?"

"I'm on assignment. We're doing some training down there in Honduras and Nicaragua."

I realized that the man behind me was going to work with the Contras. I was on my way to help the Sandinistas, he was on his way to train their killers.

The idea that I was on a plane with this reprehensible creature made me sick to my stomach. A pang of morbid curiosity made me want to look at his face, so I got up and walked to the lavatory. He was tall and young and his neat appearance was being challenged by a mess of curly hair that refused to follow orders. The stupid guy in front of me didn't look dangerous but I knew he was. I wanted to remember his face in case I ever saw him again. I hoped I never would.

3/31/86, Monday

On the flight from Houston to Nicaragua I finally dozed a bit but I never really fell asleep, so I arrived in Managua groggy, somewhat dazed and sticky after a passenger spilled her orange juice on me. I hate being sticky.

Managua airport is tiny, the size of a small town airport in the U.S. but it was teeming with soldiers, all carrying automatic rifles. I was already disoriented and this was completely intimidating to me. I'm not used to being interrogated by armed soldiers. It snapped me into the reality of this place. This is a country at war.

I walked out into the waiting area hoping to see a representative from the school but nobody was there. I walked all over the small airport but I couldn't find any Escuela Nica personnel and after a while I started to worry that the whole school for internationalists was one big scam and that now I'd be stranded in a foreign country where I didn't know a soul.

I sat on a bench, waiting and hoping someone would show up. I felt like I was dreaming but I started to plan what I would do if I had to make it work on my own. I figured I could grab a taxi and get myself to a hotel and then try to sort it out, luckily the rep from Escuela Nica finally did show up. He was half an hour late but I was so happy to see him that I didn't care!

Now I'm suffering from serious culture shock. Driving through Managua for the first time really makes me feel as though I haven't seen much of the world. I've been to Europe and I've traveled all over Mexico but only as a tourist going to museums or historical sites...not like this. This is not a place for tourists. Everywhere you look there are battle scars: the skeletons of bombed buildings, facades left standing over the ruins of old factories, warehouses and office buildings that have been reduced to piles of rubble. Nothing is new, everything looks ancient or on the verge of breaking down. Sidewalks crowded with people, waiting to catch a ride on buses already groaning under the burden of even more people hanging off the sides and riding on top. Hitchhikers trying to catch a ride on military trucks. And poverty everywhere.

Welcome To Hospedaje Norma!

4/1/86, Tuesday

After rounding up the Escuela Nica students and volunteers at the airport the school representative dropped us off at a place called Hospedaje Norma, a hostel like no hostel I've ever been to. It looked like someone just gathered up pieces of plywood and slapped them together to create partitions over a dirt floor. Each "dormitory" contained three to six cots, a bare lightbulb with a pull string to turn it on and off and nothing else.

Sanitary facilities are minimal as is access to electricity, even water is limited. I was surprised and somewhat disturbed to find that there was only one aluminum tumbler set atop a water jug for everyone in the hostel to drink from and that it was barely rinsed between users because water is too scarce to waste on rinsing. Water in that part of Managua is turned off two days a week (Mondays and Thursdays) in an effort to conserve it, so a much-needed shower after the long, sticky flight was out of the question because there was no running water last night.

Another surprise is that there is no toilet paper to be found anywhere or at any price. I was told, perhaps in jest, that La Prensa (the opposition's newspaper) usually ends up replacing it in the bathrooms. I don't know if that's what I've been using but the squares of newspaper can't be flushed, because they won't dissolve as easily as toilet paper so they must be thrown in a tin can located right next to the toilet, making for a terrible smell coming from the latrines. The first time I used the toilet, I automatically threw my paper into the bowl after wiping, then panicked and scooped it out with my bare hands for fear of creating plumbing problems for the whole neighborhood. To top that off, I couldn't even wash my hands properly. The water that's available for washing our hands is no more than a trickle from a community jug and there was no soap anywhere, so I was left feeling dirtier than ever.

In the morning we headed out to Esteli, about two hours north of Managua. We drove through the countryside which was quite a contrast with the city. It was green, lush and pristine - nature again proving its superiority over the man-made. We went straight to the Nica school where we would have the opportunity to meet the school staff, get to know our fellow students and later that afternoon, there would be a small ceremony to introduce us to our host families.

The introductory ceremony was arranged so that we would feel as comfortable as possible with families who would essentially be adopting us for the next month or so. I was greeted by my "new" little sister Lissette, a young girl with close-cropped hair and jovial, mischievous eyes. She has beautiful dark skin and a beaming smile. She greeted me warmly and apologized for the fact that her mother couldn't be there to welcome me.

Lissette was pleasantly surprised that I was not one of the students who had come to study Spanish, my fluency immediately set her at ease and she began to joke with me. I'm so glad they sent her, I can't think of a more welcoming person. We walked back to our house and Lissette insisted on pulling my wheeled suitcase through the cobblestone streets of Esteli. Along the way she asked questions and pointed out places of interest. By coincidence, we happen to have the same interest: sweets!

"There's a store near your school that sells snacks and ice cream," she informed me. "Sometimes they have banana splits. Have you ever had a banana split?"

"Yes," I started to say but she interrupted me.

"They take guineo and cut it in half and then they put ice cream in the middle..." she proceeded with her enthusiastic description but I was still back at guineo.

"What is guineo?" I asked.

"You don't know guineo? It's a fruit that's long and yellow and it tastes sweet and creamy..."

"We call that platano or banana in English."

"Oh, so you've had it before?" she asked, crestfallen that she wasn't initiating me into the delights of an unfamiliar fruit.

"Yes, but I wouldn't mind having one with you," I said, tossing her a side glance. Her smile came back.

We'd gone about five blocks when I noticed Lissette struggling with the heavy suitcase so I asked for a turn pulling it. She resisted but finally gave in, shrugging her shoulders and handing me the handle reluctantly, as though doing me a favor. I became acutely aware of how many notebooks, crayons, pencils, markers, rulers and erasers were in the overstuffed bag and I worried that one of the two little wheels would give and break off. Now that her hands were free,

Lissette switched into full tourist guide mode, pointing out places of interest to her.

"That place makes posicle, have you ever had posicle?" she asked.

"No, what is it?"

"Oh, it's hard to describe, I'll have to bring you back so you can taste it." She gave me the smile of a kid about to put her hand in a cookie jar. 'Very clever,' I thought to myself, happy to have an accomplice. A little further down the road we passed a fresh juice bar which sells freshly squeezed fruit drinks they call frescos along with pastries. Lissette's face was full of expression as she described her favorite treats. We were going to get along just fine.

My Nicaraguan Family
Front row left to right: Paca, Milche, Carelia,
Back row: Francie, Lissette, Magda

4/2/86, Wednesday

I wasn't able to shower in Managua and last night it was too late
when I finally got to our house in Esteli. Plus, everyone wanted
to get to know me and I wanted to talk to them so I waited. This
morning I finally got my shower. It was a chilly experience. The
water never got warm so I took about a one minute shower,
soaping up my entire body before turning on the cold stream for
a frigid rinse. Despite these things and many other inconveniences
of living with people at this level of poverty, I'm very glad to be
here. It's not that big a deal to have to do without the luxuries we
have back home. Oddly, having to adapt so quickly makes me feel
like an alarm clock went off in my body and soul. It's like my whole
being took a cold shower.

Yesterday I was introduced to my Nicaraguan family. It's an all
female household. Five daughters live at home and one lives in

Managua. The girls all work together to manage the house until their mom gets home from work.

Adrianna is the youngest of six daughters. She's quite thin, sweet, playful and soft spoken. She has a wild mane of messy, curly hair. I'm guessing that she's about 7 years old.

Next is Milche, she is only a little older than Adrianna, she's quiet, reserved, and very attentive.

Lissette, who picked me up yesterday at the Nica school, is the middle daughter. I find her charming and outgoing... a little rebel.

After that is Paca, she's just a teenager but she's cultivated a maternal attitude towards the younger girls and they definitely take direction from her.

Carelia is a beautiful, young high school age lady. She's not that interested in dealing with her younger sisters, probably because she has a boyfriend named Lenin who Lissette says takes up all of her time. (He already came by to say hello.)

Magda doesn't live at home, she's the oldest daughter. She's married and lives in Managua.

My Nicaraguan mother's name is Francisca Dormus Zea but I heard one of the neighbors call her Francie and I like that better. I mentioned the nickname and she insisted I call her that. She's in her mid to late thirties, a former guerrilla, with a stern countenance. Yesterday, when she first walked up to greet me she had a serious look on her face but it only took a couple of seconds for it to break into a smile. She apologized for working late and it dawned on me that she was probably just tired. We enjoyed a simple dinner of beans and tortillas and then she and I sat in the living room to talk. She wanted to know everything about me but as I told it, I found my story to be rather dull. I wanted to hear her story and after a while she shared it.

Francie is a strong, well-informed, intelligent woman with incredible vitality. She's part of a women's military reserve battalion but a lot of her time is spent doing what she calls social work. I don't know if she's an actual social worker but it sounds like she's mostly concerned with the welfare of women, making sure their needs and interests are addressed. As I listened to her, I could tell that she cares deeply about making sure that women feel involved and participate in the revolution.

Alice, Lenin and Francie

"It would be very easy for women to fall back into traditional roles," she tells me. "Many of the women in Esteli were active in trying to overthrow Somoza but to different degrees and in different ways. For those of us who were integrated in the struggle, it allowed us to see ourselves in a new way. During the seventies, women combatientes were risking their lives, the same as the men soldiers. We thought of ourselves as equals but even though we were doing the same things they were doing, we still had to put up with machismo from other soldiers, husband, brothers..."

Her voiced trailed off and I wondered if she was remembering a particular macho comment that might have wounded her. Francie sat quietly in front of me, dressed in an olive drab shirt and pants. Her legs were spread open in front of her in a pose that I had always associated with men, her body relaxed and open, completely in control of her presence and ready to act at any moment. There was a hardness to her look but a quality of gentleness in her eyes. I studied her face, noticing her earrings and a hint of lipstick. I saw a woman for whom strength and femininity were whatever she wanted them to be. She gazed off into the distance for a minute, temporarily lost in thought.

I said nothing to break the silence. Finally, she sighed and smiled at me. I wanted to know more about this matriarch but I instinctively knew not to pry.

My Nicaraguan family has been very involved (or integrated, as they say here) in the revolutionary and post-revolutionary movements. They are a rich source of history and firsthand information. Even the house we're living in seems to have a story to tell. It was used as a Sandinista headquarters and some of the leaders lived here while in Esteli. We were still seated in the living room when I happened to look at the painting that was hanging behind Francie's head. It seemed religious at first glance but there was something off about it.

"Is that a picture of Jesus?" I asked, standing to take a closer look.

The lean, dark-skinned, bearded man in the painting had a rifle dangling by his side but there was a look of peace emanating from his eyes and he appeared to have a bright amber halo over his head.

Francie laughed. "In Nicaragua, even Jesus carries a rifle."

Jesus with a rifle

4/3/86, Thursday

This morning Adrianna, the youngest of my little Nicaraguan sisters, took me on a trek to a school across town to distribute some of the supplies I collected in the U.S. The school is called Jose Benito Escobar, after a guerrilla combatant who was murdered by Somoza's Guardia here in Esteli. Adrianna told me that Comandante Escobar used to live in the house where our family lives now. We delivered our supplies to some very happy teachers who promised to put them to good use. The school was not yet open, so we didn't hang out for long. We also knew that we had a long walk back and the sun was already beating down on us. On the way back we stopped for some "gaseosas" (as carbonated drinks are called here), it was a nice treat for Adrianna. I'm amazed that someone so young knows her way around town. I must learn from her. She never complained about the heat or the fact that our sweaty skin was the perfect surface for the dust to adhere.

When we got home, I made the mistake of postponing my shower in hopes that the water would warm up by early afternoon but it was unexpectedly turned off. Now that the water's off, I guess I'll have to stay dusty until tomorrow. There is water rationing here, just like in Managua but I haven't figured out the dates and my family says it's not uncommon for it to be turned off without warning.

Paca, looking confident and beautiful

This morning I folded some clothes with my teenage sister Paca while she did the ironing. It was our first time alone together and felt like a perfect opportunity to chat. I noticed that she had some torn magazine pages taped on the wall. Among them was a photo of a woman wearing a gray head scarf and a plain gray work smock; next to it was a page from a fashion magazine featuring a woman with a huge mane of curly blonde hair. The two photos seemed incongruous next to each other, so I asked her about them. She started telling me about her trip to Cuba. She said she was rethinking how she defined beauty and explained that at one point, her wall had been covered with images from magazines of women whose lifestyles had nothing to do with hers, like the one of the woman with blonde hair. They were images from the same magazines I had grown up with, which featured predominately Caucasian women in expensive clothes.

Paca carefully ironed the cuffs on Lissette's Bermuda shorts, made sure the fold on both legs was even, and continued with her story.

"I like their straight hair, but mine has very tight curls." She twisted a curl between her fingers. "And their skin looks so smooth."

"They never have mosquito bites!" I added, scratching one of mine.

"Their skin is milky white, like they've never gone out in the sun."

"Maybe they haven't. It takes a lot of work to look like that."

"My mom says they alter the photographs to make them look perfect."

"They do," I reassured her.

Then Paca dropped a bomb. "But why is THAT considered perfect?" She pointed at the big-haired blonde. I had never considered that question. I knew the standards were impossible but I never wondered who set them or why certain features were considered beautiful. I was momentarily sent back to my childhood, remembering adults in East L.A. cooing over a child with guerito features. Kids could be ugly as sin but if they had light skin, eyes or hair they would receive heaps of praise. I had never understood it.

Paca finished with Lissette's shorts, moved on to Francie's uniform pants and meticulously creased them. Taking the tip of the iron, she gently tapped each pleat with it, pressing love into her family's clothing, enacting the type of beauty she knows she possesses, the type that is now on her wall - the beauty that comes from a sense of purpose.

"When I went to Cuba, I saw women who looked more like me. They were beautiful. They were average working women, not models," Paca said. "It was my mom's idea to put up the picture of the factory worker. Now, when I see images like this one," she gestured to the ultra-thin, airbrushed model, "I realize I can never look like them and I'm starting to understand that that's okay."

Beauty in fashion magazines does not reflect or validate the average working woman, especially if the woman is not Caucasian. Learning to accept an appearance that is seldom validated takes ongoing conscious effort. The pressure intensifies as we get older when not only your ethnicity or body type can be portrayed as unattractive but when the natural process of aging is depicted as something ugly that needs to be avoided or corrected

When it comes to the household, Paca is second in command. She organizes the kids to help with the chores when Francie is at work. The whole family pitches in, since Francie is the sole breadwinner and it takes teamwork to keep things running smoothly. Paca cooks most of the meals when Francie is away. Yesterday, she cooked a very strange dinner for us, a big bowl of mashed tubers that looked like purpley-gray mashed potatoes. I'm not sure what it was called. We all ate it even though it was rather bland.

Lissette helps with the laundry

Noticing that I hadn't eaten much, Lissette took the opportunity to introduce me to posicle. We walked a few blocks to an ordinary looking house with no signage. Lissette knocked and after a few minutes an older woman cracked the door open and peeked at us.

"*Hay Posicle?*" Lissette inquired.

The old woman smiled and opened the door all the way to reveal a waist high freezer. "*Si hay,*" she replied in a friendly manner. I still wasn't sure what we were getting. Posicle sounded a lot like Popsicle and the freezer seemed to confirm my suspicions but I was willing to be surprised. I gave Lissette the money and let her order for us. She handed the money to the woman who gave her two plastic sandwich bags with something reddish purple frozen inside. We thanked the woman and said goodbye.

Lissette handed me the Posicle. I stared at it.

"I'll show you how to eat it," she said. She grabbed a corner of the Baggie, squeezed and twisted it to create a sort of handle, then she bit off the opposite corner of the plastic bag and spit it out onto the street. I followed her example. "Now you just suck it out through that corner."

"What is it?" I asked.

"Frozen Grape Punch" she said immediately, putting the corner of the bag in her mouth.

"You said it was hard to describe," I teased.

"Well…I thought I should show you how to eat it," she smiled.

Later that evening, she showed me how to eat banana sorbets.

It's not always easy finding stuff to snack on, which is trying for someone like me who's used to grazing all day. It seems like one of the most popular Nicaraguan sayings is *no hay* (there isn't any.) You walk up to a cafe and they'll have a chalkboard out front with that day's offerings, except that as the day progresses, you tend to find no hay handwritten next to many items. Often, they don't even bother with the *"no hay"*, you sit down thinking you'll order something that caught your eye and you're stuck with Gallo Pinto… again! The one thing there is plenty of is sugar. Nicaraguans eat more sugar than even a sweet freak like me can handle. It typically comes in the form of frescos, which are usually just a combination of fruit, sugar and water. My favorite fresco is avena, which is a finely ground oatmeal that is soaked in sugar water and cinnamon, it's sooooo good!

I wonder if consuming all that fresco makes one's blood sweeter. Well, at least I know the mosquitos are eating well! If it wasn't for the mosquito net, I'd have been eaten alive. Just now, as I've started to complain about the mosquitos, I spied a visitor in my room. I don't want to be a baby about this but there's a big lizard crawling on the wall and I'm scared. I'm going to try to ignore it, maybe it'll leave soon...hmm, it's not leaving. I guess I'm going to go read in the other room for a little while. I've been lent lots of books and I haven't had time to read them.

Lorraine Scognamillo, 2015

4/3/86PM, Thursday

I wait in the classroom where there are five chairs and four tables of assorted heights, shapes and sizes. Soon students of all ages, from children to adults start to trickle in. They greet each other warmly. Some carry chairs, the early birds snag one of the five available chairs, while others resign themselves to a lesson on foot.

A man in coveralls has apparently come straight from work. His clothes and hands look dirty but no one seems to mind. A woman comes in with an infant in her arms and a little girl pulling at her skirt. One of the early birds offers her his chair but she declines, choosing instead to sway with her baby at the back of the room while the little girl goes out to play with some of the other children who are waiting for their parents to attend class.

This group is on Lesson Ten. The teacher writes the following sentence on the board: *La reforma agraria recupera la producción de la tierra para el pueblo.* (Agrarian reform recovers the land for the use of the people.) She reads aloud, then the students join her. Discussion ensues as she reminds the class that they are waiting for everyone to get there. I walk around, eavesdropping on the little groups clustered around the tables. Some are discussing the sentence, others are still catching up with each other about what happened during their day.

After a while, the little classroom is full and dialogue fills every corner. The woman with the baby joins a round table, still swaying as she interjects with her opinions. The teacher reads the sentence again, placing an open palm under each word as she reads it. *"La reforma agraria recupera la producción de la tierra para el pueblo."* Some of the students join her, others just listen. Then she asks if anyone has any comments about the sentence. One man jokes, "I didn't know I'd been robbed until right now!" Other joking comments follow and then more serious observations about Somocismo, about which types of crops are most beneficial. Everyone who wants to speak is given the opportunity. Differing views are expressed but the feeling of mutual respect is always there, modeled by the teacher and followed by the students.

Soon the teacher leads the class back to the sentence and underlines the word recupera. The class reads it. She breaks it into syllables and pronounces each one, again placing her palm under each syllable as she reads it, re-cu-pe-ra. The class joins her. Next she underlines the syllable re. She makes the sounds of the letter r, gently rolling it off her tongue.

"What other vowels can we combine with this letter?" she asks the class.

The woman with the infant quickly calls out "ru-ru-ru!" The class bursts into laughter as the ru-ru-ru sound is often made by mothers who are trying to coax their babies to sleep. Her baby has just started to make soft, whimpering sounds.

"Ru, ru, ru! Con u, u, u," the teacher calls back. The formal phonics lesson continues as the new syllables are constructed with the previously introduced consonant and vowels.

It makes a lot of sense to me to have the students go from understanding the meaning of a sentence and how that message pertains to their lives to breaking down the words into syllables and letters. They understand the power of written language to transmit ideas. To learn to read and write is to harness that power.

Even after the class is over, the dialogue component of the lesson has a lasting effect. Some of the students linger to chat, eager for the opportunity to share their ideas. The subject of discussion is not limited to the contents of the primer, it only begins there. Individual, community, national, and international concerns are all valid subjects for discussion and collective actions are encouraged. Everyone is expected to exchange viewpoints in a setting that encourages respect, fosters community and promotes praxis, breaking down the separation between theory and practice.

I have just one gripe. Despite the fact that the ruling party - the FSLN - is extremely popular, the party is too repeatedly mentioned in the school books in comparison with opposition parties who are rarely (if ever) mentioned at all. I think it's important to have balance and consider different points of view. The problem is that the coalition of armed forces that opposed Somoza banded together under the name FSLN but after they overthrew him, the coalition disbanded and formed different parties with divergent political and economic ideologies. They all opposed Somoza and that had forced them to work together but once he was gone, the differences between them became evident, so the FSLN of a few years ago is a different entity from the FSLN today.

Nonetheless, the literacy program is impressively efficient. It has a wonderful success rate and I believe there are many aspects of it which I can implement in my own teaching back home.

Audrey at the fresco shop

4/4/86, Friday

I've been hanging out with Audrey a lot. She's one of the students at Escuela NICA. I like that she seems happy and eager to fill a room with her raspy laugh. We're going through a similar journey, both of us are amazed at how far we've come since we first got here. She also saved me from myself. One of the women at the school started to give me a derisive smirk when she saw me applying colored lip balm but before I had a chance to snap at her, Audrey came over and asked to borrow it. Carrie, the smirk-giver quipped, "You two always have to look good, don't you?"

Audrey laughed at her good-naturedly and I responded "we don't have to, we just can't help it." Audrey is cute, she has short, auburn hair and a thin frame and neither of us wears much more than tinted lip balm and mosquito repellent. Carrie doesn't wear make-up or deodorant and she brags about it as though it somehow strengthens her political views. She's not always annoying but she sometimes acts like a know-it-all. She goes around correcting people's Spanish pronunciation but she's not even a teacher, she's just another student. She doesn't ever correct my Spanish, she'd better not even try.

Audrey and I have learned to deal with the bugs, lizards, and rats. We've learned to eat food we'd never even heard of before. We've compromised our own standards of sanitation. We've learned to sleep through the clucking of the hens, the crowing of the roosters, and the pigeons walking and cooing on the tins roofs overhead.

This morning, I saw a woman walking a cute little black pig on a leash. Its legs were moving really fast and the woman was having a hard time keeping up. Before I could take out my camera, the woman and the pig were halfway down the street. Chickens and pigs are everywhere, they walk along the road with everyone else. I have noticed that there are no homeless people or beggars to be seen. I don't know if they exist, everyone seems to have some kind of job.

I brought some cheap, lightweight tennis shoes that I wear at work, thinking they would be perfect for walking, but they are no match for the sett paved streets of Esteli. I think I packed inadequately. Contact lenses, make up and sweaters are out of the question, I wish I had a good pair of walking shoes and toilet paper instead. This afternoon the water was cut off unexpectedly. I was really thirsty and decided to go to the market to buy some soda, maybe even rescue the family from another meal of beans and rice, which incidentally, we have eaten everyday since I got here.

When I got to the store, I noticed that many of the shelves were empty. There were some bottles of hot sauce, dry beans, dry rice, a small selection of ugly looking vegetables, a few household items and very little else. Everything was inexpensive. I asked the woman behind the counter about the scarce selection. She informed me

Kelly Thompson, 2015

that when something is in stock, it is cheap enough that anyone can buy it and so it sells out quickly.

"The US has declared an embargo against us, but they will not break us. We'll eat beans forever if we have to." There was disapproval in the woman's voice. "You are a guest in this country. You do not buy the groceries." It suddenly struck me that what I was doing was rude. Who did I think I was, coming to their country, thinking I could buy better food because I had more money? I felt stupid and decided against the groceries and asked her for some toilet paper instead.

"*Papel hygienico?*"

She looked amused. "*No hay.* Go back to your family and live like a Nicaraguan."

4/5/86, Saturday

Last night we had a frightening experience. Some time between 11:00 pm and midnight, we heard machine gun fire going off somewhere in town. The shooting continued erratically for about an hour while I lay in my bed, feeling scared. I thought the town was under siege. I had to pee desperately but I have to go outside to get to the bathroom, so despite the fact that I was terrified of leaving my bedroom, I quietly walked outside and then tiptoed back again. After awhile, the shooting died down and I was able to sleep a little but I had a pretty good scare.

This morning, nobody seemed to be quite sure what the machine gun fire was all about. My Nicaraguan mother, Francie says she got up and got dressed in case we had to evacuate in a hurry. She is perplexed, she says it may have just been a *bolo* (drunk) having war flashbacks. Luckily, two of my little sisters slept through the incident. Anyway, the real attack came from the bugs. I'm covered with bug bites despite the sleeping bag, repellent, and mosquito netting. C'est la vie.

Comandante Gladys Baez

4/6/86, Sunday

Today started off a lazy day, playing cards at a neighbor's house. When I got home, I found that Francie had company. She had a friend over, Comandante Gladys Baez of the Sandinista armed forces, a short woman with indigenous features who wore her hair in braids. She looked more like someone getting ready to bake a batch of cookies than lead an army. She was really warm and friendly and kissed me on the cheek when she met me.

Comandante Baez insisted that I call her Gladys and seemed surprised when Francie said I was American. Gladys complimented me on my Spanish and Francie agreed, saying I acted, looked and spoke like a Nica, which I know she meant as a big compliment. I took it as one. We sat down in the living room to talk. Gladys asked me about life in the United States and what people in the U.S. thought of the war between the Contras and Sandinistas. I confirmed the things she already knew, that Reagan was on a campaign to change public opinion of the counterrevolutionary Contras by talking them up as patriots who are protecting us from the spread of communism and by refusing to use the word Contra and employing instead the sympathetic sounding name "Freedom Fighters" when referring to them. I told her that it was working. Furthermore, they were now being described as advisors rather than combatants, something that the Nicaraguans knew was a blatant lie.

Gladys moved on from the topic of Reagan and asked me about women in my country. That was hard for me to talk about. It seems that the death of the Equal Rights Amendment has stalled any progress for the women's movement. I don't understand what happened with the ERA and I can't explain it to her, I guess I'm just too far removed from the mainstream. I told her I was involved in music and that my musician friends were generally open-minded about politics and women's rights. I said that the kind of music I play has been liberating for women because it's more about having something to say than being a great musician. So women, even those who were novice musicians, were not intimidated or shut out due to lack of experience. She was happy to hear that more women were playing music and writing songs and encouraged me to write a song about Nicaragua and share the experiences I was having here with my friends back home. She didn't seem much older than me but she took on a motherly tone as she reminded me that "*Sin la mujer, no hay revolucion.*" (Without equality for women, there is no revolution). I'd never heard anyone say this before, despite the fact that it seemed like such a simple and obvious truth.

Later, when Gladys had left, I had to ask Francie again if I had heard correctly. Was Gladys really a comandante? I guess if I tried hard, I could imagine her as a guerrilla but a comandante? She didn't look or act like a warrior, much less a commander. I couldn't imagine her bossing the men around. She looked like so many women in East L.A., ordinary working class moms and tias. My Nicaraguan mother assured me that Gladys was one of the first and most respected Sandinista comandantes. She laughed at me and asked why I doubted her. I said that I didn't think Gladys looked strong enough to be taken seriously as a comandante.

"Why don't you think she's strong?" Francie asked.

"Oh, I don't know," I lied.

I was too ashamed to say it was because I expected muscles and a snazzy uniform; inwardly, I had to admit that I expected a man. I had never seen a woman who looked like Gladys have any power. In my world, women who looked like Gladys took care of kids, did housework, warmed up tortillas. I glimpsed myself just for a second in all my sexist, racist and colorist ugliness and I quickly stepped away from the mirror.

Francie cocked her head, looked up at me and said, "Es MUY fuerte. She fought alongside (FSLN Founder) Carlos Fonseca," she assured me. Francie went on to tell me a little about what she and Gladys had done together. They were pioneers in AMNLAE (Asociación de Mujeres Nicaragüenses, Luisa Amanda Espinoza) an organization which is named after the first female casualty in the war against Somoza. Espinoza escaped a life of poverty and abuse to become a revolutionary. Originally, the organization was to address the needs and concerns of women who were fighting to overthrow Somoza; now, it is dedicated to increasing the political participation of women in post-revolutionary Nicaragua. Francie and Gladys were not only active members, they were founding members.

"Gladys herself was tortured by Somoza's Guardia," Francie continued. "She was captured by Somoza and held prisoner for over two months in solitary confinement. She never broke down."

I imagine this braided woman in an interrogation room, bright lights shining in her face, electrodes shocking her as she refuses to talk. Sweat runs down her lovely, weather-worn face, where a look of strength and resolve is carved deeper than Mt. Rushmore. Unexpectedly, a man and some snot-nosed kids look into the interrogation room.

"Gladys, we need some warm tortillas," they call to her.

"Heat your own damn tortillas!" she replies. "Can't you see I'm busy?"

Seeds for Germination:

Years later, when I embarked on my book tour to promote Violence Girl, my bassist and I were two middle aged women in our fifties, touring and playing punk. I had serious insecurities about booking a DIY book tour, sleeping on couches, floors or rehearsal rooms. I still hadn't fully realized the lesson of what strength looks like and where it comes from. In the end, my desire to tell people about my book made my fears and insecurities irrelevant and showed me that I was capable of more than I believed.

4/7/86, Monday

I woke up very early this morning and after a big cup of thick black coffee and a bowl of beans, I felt ready to go out and do some construction. A small group of us met at the NICA school where we waited for a ride to our work site out in the country. Since the school's Spanish classes are in the morning, the Spanish students would not be part of the construction brigade, but we had a few volunteers from the community and from the Salvadoran collective.

We were all in good spirits, eager to get to work but it only took a couple of hours for my little bubble to burst. I discovered that I am not cut out for masonry work. When we first got to the site, they had me laying bricks but apparently I sucked at it, so they sent me down to the bottom of a hill to fetch a load of bricks in a wheelbarrow. It was tough because the terrain was rocky and very uneven. Pushing a cart load of bricks is heavy work and frankly, I'm a little flabby these days since I haven't been going to the gym. When I hit a rock on the way up, I lost control of the cart and couldn't keep it from tipping over. All I could do was watch the bricks careen down the hillside, breaking on their way down. I felt terrible. Carrie sneered at me. I think she was secretly happy that I was proving to be the fuck-up she imagines me to be. Everyone else tried to hide their chagrined expressions, saying it was okay but I could tell they were thinking I should have stayed home.

I cleaned up my mess and went back to bricklaying after the mortar application method had been explained to me again and I seemed to do a bit better. Working out in the open air in the middle of the country is something I never thought I would like but for a few moments, standing on that green hill, breathing the cool, fresh air and watching a little posse of ragtag kids running after each other, I could understand the attraction. An hour later that charm would wear off. By midday I was sweaty, tired and hungry and even the kids didn't look as cute.

When it was time to go in and eat, I was hungry but I felt like such a poseur, I didn't think I deserved the bowl of beans and corn tortillas that I was handed. I felt certain that the money spent on the bricks I'd broken could feed this family for a week. The kids ran around barefoot with clothes that were so old they were practically transparent and the house we were eating in made the Little House on the Prairie look posh. I tried to turn down the food but the cook insisted. Obviously, she hadn't seen me drop the bricks.

Part of the value of participating in a cooperative construction project is going through the process of building relationships, it's every bit as important as the process of building a house. True, I messed up, but if others were willing to forgive me, I could have and should have forgiven myself. Indulging in self-pity is a waste of time, better to accept a mistake and try to move forward with a positive attitude.

Fuck This!

4/8/86, Tuesday

Last night was crazy! We had been at the construction site all day and the sun was already setting when the driver dropped us off at the NICA school. One of the women who runs the school invited us to her house for a glass of Flor de Caña. Hillary is an American ex-pat who's been living in Esteli for a few years now and she's been great at giving us tips on adapting to our new surroundings. She's also one of the few people here who can afford to keep alcohol handy for entertaining. Most people buy, trade or grow what they consume on a daily basis. My family doesn't even have a refrigerator. Our kitchen is a small room with a table, a stove and two small cupboards that hold salt, dry beans, and other bare necessities. The sink is outside and it's used for washing hands, clothes and dishes.

Anyway, I'm getting off track. Christie and Nancy, two of the students who are studying Spanish went with me to Hillary's for the local rum. Occasionally, if gaseosas are available, Flor de Caña is mixed with cola and lime to make a fancy Cuba Libre but tonight, we drank it warm and straight. We only had one drink before we realized it was getting late and our families would wonder where we'd gone, so we decided it was time for us to leave. Christie, whose Nicaraguan family lives way on the other side of town was afraid to walk home alone as it was well after 10 pm and quite a distance. Since Nancy and I live in the same neighborhood, we walked Christie home first before turning back toward our own houses.

We were having a great time, talking and joking along the way when we suddenly heard automatic rifle fire in the streets. We jumped over the shrubbery of a nearby house and ducked behind the bushes, our hearts pounding as we tried to calculate the proximity of the shots and whether or not they were approaching. The sound of the automatic rifles was close but didn't seem to be advancing. I was acutely aware that if someone sprayed our hiding place with bullets, the hedges would offer no protection. I crouched, thinking of hitting the ground belly first, like I've seen in dozens of action movies but as I deliberated the gun fire suddenly stopped. Nancy and I froze in our crouched positions, listening to see if anyone was coming, trying not to move, daring not to even breathe. Minutes crawled by while we looked at each other, waiting for more gun fire, preferably in the distance but it was eerily quiet, no sound coming from any of the neighborhood houses, everyone laying low. After what felt like a very long time we felt bold enough to signal and start whispering to each other, neither of us sure if it was safe to get up and start walking home again. Eventually, we worked up the nerve to resume our journey. Our easy, joking stroll a thing of the past, we became Olympic speed walkers the rest of the way home, pointing out good places to duck in case the gunshots came back.

The whole experience felt surreal: one minute we were drinking warm rum, the next we were dodging bullets. It's almost as though we have to ignore the war to continue with everyday life. It's oddly easy to forget about the war but we are in a state of emergency. The war does exist and it's all around us.

Archbishop Oscar Romero

4/9/86, Wednesday

Today I went to the Salvadoran agricultural cooperative along with three other students from the NICA school. I thought I was gonna faint! It was hot, heavy work. I was planting rows of tomatoes and hoeing little irrigation ditches. I tied a bandana around my head to keep my hair back and it was soaked with sweat within minutes. I got blisters on my hands and fingers from clutching the handle of the hoe. Every now and then, some disgusting bug would poke its head up and I'd clobber it with the hoe. The first time I saw the ugly insects I started to scream but I quickly felt embarrassed by my sissy, city-girl behavior as my co-workers communicated their annoyance with a quick glance. After that, I simply hit the bugs with the edge of my hoe, attempting to slice them in half. I felt mean doing it but they freaked me out.

Our Salvadoran co-workers are refugees from the war in El Salvador. Some of them were part of the FMLN, Farabundo Marti

Liberacion Nacional, others were denounced by *"orejas,"* informants who accuse people of conspiring to overthrow the government. Those accusations are as good as a death sentence. The FMLN is an armed guerrilla organization trying to do for El Salvador what the FSLN has done here. Our *compañeros* had to flee their country to avoid death and/or torture but they're still committed to raising awareness of their cause. Talking to them while we worked helped me take my mind off my aching body. As we listened to their stories of political repression and corruption, our minds were distracted from the physical strain. Some of these compañeros have lost family members to the struggle and all of them have lost loved ones. They talk about Bishop Romero's assassination and the subsequent massacre of mourners at his funeral by the police. I can tell that the pain is still fresh, it's generational. Their parents and grandparents have fought against *Las Catorce*, the fourteen families that made up the oligarchy for as long as they can remember so even though the heat was terrible and every inch of me ached, I felt like I could push through the work. It seemed worth the pain to help them out, to show solidarity in my own very small way.

In the evening the driver dropped us off at the school again, just in time for a charla with the Mothers of Heroes and Martyrs of the Revolution. It was heartbreaking hearing the mothers tell and probably relive the pain of their loved one's death and in some cases, their torture. Several of the stories involved gory dismemberment and my stomach turned as I thought of cutting insects in half with my hoe that day. The thought that someone could do that to a person made me sick. They took turns telling their stories until every eye at the charla was teary. At the end, one of the mothers told us that she wanted us to know what our tax dollars are doing here in Nicaragua and that although it was hard for them to talk about the terrible tragedies that had happened to their families, the purpose was for us to understand the cruelty and inhumanity being inflicted on them as a result of our government's financial and military support of the Contras. They urged us to help them change the situation. I felt so bad. How is it that they don't hate us? I want to help but how can I change it?

Archbishop Oscar Romero gained great popularity in El Salvador in the seventies when he began speaking out against poverty, social injustice and the assassination of political dissidents. His Sunday sermons were broadcast on the radio and had a far reaching effect as they provided a rallying point for disenfranchised Salvadorans.

In 1980 Romero was fatally shot while celebrating mass. His funeral was attended by over 250,000 people. The ceremony was disrupted by smoke bombs and gun shots directed at the mourners. The attack left dozens dead and hundreds wounded. It was believed that the Salvadoran government was behind the attack.

Shortly after this the country plunged into civil war.

4/10/86, Thursday

There is so much poverty here. It's hard to put into words but some of the campesinos literally dress in rags, the cloth so threadbare that it can't possibly offer much protection from the elements. They eat just a bowl of beans and a few tortillas and they have to work very, very hard just for that. I'm sure that in the U.S., we'd call their houses shacks. Many are put together with scavenged building materials from bombed or demolished sites and do not have indoor plumbing. Outhouses are common. On top of all this, the country is at war and their kids are being sent off to fight. How is it that they don't break? People smile through it. Walk by any house in Esteli and you can hear people singing at the top of their lungs while doing their chores.

Last night, we went to a party for Francie's friend, Paco. It was very interesting to see how politically aware everyone is. The party consisted of a lot of former combatientes and others who at some point were integrated in the struggle. Everyone sat around discussing internal and external affairs and, in particular, the rights of women and their participation in the revolution. I've never been to a party like that. It was so odd to hear the women telling the men exactly what they were thinking and what needed to be done to promote equal opportunity. Who talks like that at a party? In L.A., a party involves getting dressed up, getting drunk, and maybe finding someone to have sex with. Meaningful talk is optional.

I like to hear the men and women refer to each other as compañero and compañera or even the shortened compa. The word can mean partner or companion, it's so much sweeter than calling someone "Honey" or "Baby." I'd much rather be an equal partner and companion than sweet or childlike.

There was no dancing at the party, no games, no chips or dip. A compañera brought a bottle of homemade rum and I took polite sips of what I suspected was really paint thinner. Everyone drank in moderation and the general mood seemed to indicate that discussion was the best entertainment. People exchanged passionate, sometimes opposing viewpoints. They listened and reflected and offered thoughtful responses. Everyone was engaged and, once again, I had the feeling that people in this country were somehow more alive than people in the U.S. It made me sad for my country, where people get bored at parties and we often feel the need to drink before we can talk in a social setting and even then, we rarely say anything that we feel this passionately about. It seems like a heated discussion in the U.S. is considered impolite; here, it's considered stimulating.

4/11/86, Friday

We had two charlas in Managua today. The first one at the American embassy was a waste of time since the embassy spokesperson just repeated U.S. President Reagan's position of alleged human rights violations by the Sandinistas. I felt like every word he uttered was measured and delivered like bullet points off a memo. The second charla was with journalist Mark Cook at the Latin American Historical Institute and was much more informative, interesting and relaxed. He struck me as a reliable source of information. Following an overview of the country's history, Mark surprised us with the news that Reagan is still trying to secure 100 million dollars in aid for the contras. This, despite the fact that Congress has forbidden this type of assistance. I don't know how Reagan plans to get around the Congressional ban but if he manages to do it, it could be devastating for the Sandinista government.

The Iran-Contra Affair

Around the same time that I was writing this entry, some interesting things were happening in the United States. President Reagan had authorized the CIA to begin financing, arming and training the Contras (or counter-revolutionaries), most of whom were the remnants of Somoza's National Guard. During this time, a majority of Americans were opposed to funding the overthrow of the Nicaraguan government. In 1982, Congress passed the Boland Amendment to prevent the U.S. from providing any military assistance to forces attempting to overthrow the Sandinistas, thus blocking Reagan's funding for the Contras.

The Reagan administration sought to circumvent the restrictions. A clandestine plan was devised whereby arms would be sold via Israel to Iran, which at the time was subject to an arms embargo following their own Islamic revolution and overthrow of the pro-West Reza Shah Pahlavi. The illegal arms sale was presumably meant to facilitate the release of American hostages held by the Iranian Ayatollah Khomeini (although Ronald Reagan vehemently denied that there had ever been any arms for hostages deal.) With the help of NSA Lt. Col. Oliver North, a large portion of proceeds from the arms sales were diverted to fund the Contras. A Lebanese newspaper broke the story and The Iran-Contra Affair became a scandal for the Reagan administration. Ronald Reagan appointed the Tower Commission to look into it, but the investigation was impeded by withholding and deliberate destruction of evidence.

After Mark's presentation, we broke off into small brainstorming groups. We face the daunting task of figuring out how a handful of freelance journalists and volunteers can provide an alternate narrative that will counteract Reagan's propaganda machine. The journalists can quickly write an article and communicate with their readers. I don't have that type of forum and I find it difficult to imagine how I'm going to turn this experience into something that can change people's minds.

At night, we went out dancing at a place called Lobo Jack. It was very Americanized, lots of internationalists drinking a lot. I talked to Mark about the possibility of doing something with Gladys Baez. It would be great to have her visit the United States, meet women, and talk about her experiences in the revolution. I don't know if I have what it takes to organize speaking dates for her. I still have a bad taste in my mouth after trying to organize that benefit for the Mexican earthquake victims. That one was so poorly attended, I felt embarrassed to hand the check to the Red Cross representative at the end of the night. What if we raise money to take Gladys out to California and people don't show up? It was just an idea but I'll have to think about whether it's something I can deliver.

> *Accepting defeat before even attempting something is a lazy way out. It saves work but robs us of the opportunity to succeed and to challenge our perceived limitations or to fail miserably and thus learn from the experience.*

Fuck This!

Mark and I bonded quickly over music, he is a Buzzcocks fan and very easy to talk to, so I told him about my difficulty finding meaningful solidarity work.

"I heard about the bricks," he said.

"Does everybody know?" I was so embarrassed. Ignoring my question, he suggested that I might be more helpful doing something I'm good at and that I enjoy. What a good idea, why didn't I think of that? I'll talk to the school about going back to the art collective to volunteer there when I'm not doing literacy.

4/12/86, Saturday

Last night at Lobo Jack, I talked to a lot of people. Many of us have reached a point in this journey where we understand that it's time to move past learning the truth, it's time to start acting on it.

I feel more in tune with humanity down here. Talking to the internationalists, hearing about their work, makes me appreciate the courage of those who take action. I realize that I spend a lot of time in my head, exploring ideas instead of doing anything. Ideas should be utilized, they shouldn't rot in your head like uneaten fruit on a vine. I have to stop being stupid, thinking that planting tomatoes on an agricultural cooperative is going to make any great change in those people's lives; it probably only made a difference in mine.

I've been offered a teaching job in the mountains just north of Esteli. It's dangerous territory. The closer you get to Honduras, the closer you get to the fighting, but the children have been in desperate need of teachers for a while. I'm considering it. I could be happy here. I've fallen in love with this country and these people, despite the poverty and the hardship.

I still remember my first night, scooping paper out of the toilet with my hand for fear of screwing up the whole neighborhood's plumbing. Hearing the roosters crow even at night, being exposed to third world living conditions for the first time in my life, finding out that it wasn't uncommon for people to live in boarded up shacks with little or no plumbing; in fact, it was the norm. I remember the first week, getting used to the unannounced water shutoffs, seeing people riding horses on the streets right next to cars, getting used to not having a refrigerator or washing machine, learning to use a scrub board, learning to take bucket baths, learning to tuck the mosquito netting so the little suckers couldn't sneak in under the net; learning what it means to be Nicaraguan. God, I love this place.

I love my own country too, and I miss home and my loved ones and my band. I could also make a difference there, it's just not as easy to see what needs to be done. There are children who need a bilingual teacher like me in Los Angeles but I can't abandon Nicaragua. I don't know what to do.

4/13/86, Sunday

This afternoon, I was sitting on my bed, admiring the welts on my legs, fighting the urge to scratch my mosquito bites when I saw my 7 year-old sister Adrianna peeking at me. She gave a little shiver when she saw that I had caught her spying on me.

"Do they hurt?" she eeked in the tiniest voice, her thin frame seemed to provide no resonance.

"Yes! They're driving me crazy!" I said, eager to share my misery with anyone who would listen.

"I know something that will fix it." She took a seat at the bottom of the two concrete steps leading into my room. I was on the edge of the bed looking out at her, thinking how small she was, this sweet little mouse who claimed to have the answer to my problems.

"You do? What is it?"

She smiled at me mysteriously. "You have to come with me and I'll show you."

I looked at her for a minute. Her hair was a wind-blown cloud of brown curls that bounced over her shoulders, a wild child but so quiet. The sun was starting to go down and I knew we had very little time before the next mosquito attack would begin, so I made a quick decision. "OK, let's go!" Adrianna told Paca she was going out with me and that we'd be back in less than an hour. We walked out the door and away from town, passing the drug store and the market along the way.

"Where are we going? They don't have it in town?" I asked.

Adriana smiled at me like she was looking at an imbecile. "No, they don't have it in the store. You don't have to buy anything." She kept looking at me slyly, smiling but saying nothing as we continued on our trek. Every now and then she would nod or shake her head in response to my questions but she was obviously focused and my babbling didn't interest her. Soon we were on the road out of town. It was flanked by green fields with wild plants, weeds and grass. I looked down at my petite, enigmatic companion and realized we were looking for herbs to make a poultice for my legs. I pointed out plants as we walked, trying to be helpful. I started to doubt her. After all, she was a very young child who might not know exactly what she was looking for.

"Is it that one?" I said, pointing out different plants.

"No," she answered repeatedly. Then I saw a glimmer in her eyes. "I think we found it," she said gleefully. I followed her gaze to a strange looking weed that was growing next to a giant cow turd. She ran over to it. Ignoring the weed, she stood and beamed, pointing down at the cow turd. Was this a joke? Did she bring me all the way out here to play a trick on me? I was still looking at her when to my amazement she bent over and started to pick up the poop.

"NO!" I screamed at her. "Don't touch it!"

She laughed at me. "It's ok, it's dry," she picked up a stick and tapped the turd with it so that I could hear it. A big crap meringue.

"Wait, how is this going to help?"

"You'll see," she said, walking back toward the house with the cow pie in hand, oblivious to my concerns.

My mind was reeling. She had picked up poop with her bare hands. I was going to be in so much trouble if Francie found out that I hadn't prevented this horrible insult to hygiene. I'd wash and sterilize her hands somehow when we got home. I ran to catch up with her, continuing to protest and question her as we walked but she kept giving me her closed mouth smile. I was still an imbecile to her. Did she think she was going to get me to make a poultice of cow shit and pat it on my legs? I wasn't that desperate...or was I?

"Let's just forget it, Adrianna. Let's leave it here," I pleaded. But she ignored me and kept on walking. When we got home, I saw to my dismay that Francie was already back from work. She and Paca saw what Adrianna was carrying and smiled at us. They didn't think we were crazy. This was not a joke. Francie grabbed a box of long wooden matches and Adrianna led our little procession back to my doorway where she set the cow pie down on the steps and proceeded to light it on fire. It burned slowly, like incense. A long, smokey serpent danced its way into my room.

"The smoke will help keep the mosquitos away, " Francie said. Paca, Adrianna, and Francie all looked at me, now they all wore the smile.

Maybe I am an imbecile. But there will be no mosquitos in my room tonight.

Adrianna and the cow pie

4/14/86, Monday

Whew, what a scare! Sometime this morning between 12:30 and 1:00, machine gun fire startled us awake. The rounds were going off nonstop for about half an hour. It sounded like a battle was happening somewhere in the town. Francie got up to check on the girls but they were all asleep. She came to my room and we sat quietly listening to the gunfire.

Francie thought the Contras might be trying to take control of the electricity tower which seemed to be the direction from where the gunfire was coming. I asked Francie whether we should wake up the girls, but she said no, not unless we absolutely had to. She and I were dressed and between us we figured we could help the girls get into their jackets and shoes in a hurry if it came to it. Even after the gunfire stopped, Francie and I stayed up for about another hour, unable to calm down enough to go back to bed but eventually she insisted that we both try to get some sleep.

This morning I heard Francie talking to one of our neighbors about the sleepless night. I went out to join them when another neighbor walked by and overheard our conversation. She assured us that last night's gunfire had not been a battle but a reenactment of the April insurrection that happened in 1979. Francie became a little angry, saying that they should have made sure everyone knew and I agree with her. Several other families hadn't known and had also been frightened.

Today, the Barricada (the local newspaper) came out with a big article on the anniversary of the battle. My friend and neighbor Freddy has his picture in the paper in one of the combat scenes. The mood in the neighborhood quickly shifted from anger at not knowing about last night's battle reenactment to pride in having our neighbor Freddy featured in the newspaper.

La Chacara prison

4/15/86, Tuesday

Last night, I went to the movies with Audrey and my little sister Adrianna. It was a terrible, scratchy print of a James Bond movie with Spanish subtitles. The print was so bad that I lost interest and feel asleep. When they woke me up at the end of the movie I realized that I'd been attacked by fleas. That's what I get for wearing a skirt and forgetting my Off! My legs were covered with itchy bug bites. When we got home from the movie, Adrianna came to my room to tuck me in. Not my blankets - it's too hot for that - but she wanted to ensure that the mosquito netting was tucked in on all side so that nothing could fly in and bite me while I slept. She is so sweet.

This morning we visited the Chacara Penitentiary. I was impressed with the conditions in the prison. Everything was very clean, the prisoners seemed healthy and the majority of them were engaged in productive work. The Chacara provides opportunity for the prisoners to become involved in the prison's incentive program whereby they earn credits through work and education. Most prisoners take advantage of the program.

There are literacy classes for prisoners to attain functional literacy: levels 1, 2 and 3. If the prisoners master those levels, there are opportunities for them to attend outside schools by special permission, provided they have a history of good behavior. All prisoners who work receive a salary and they're trained in marketable skills that will allow them to gain employment when they are released from prison. Conjugal visits and weekend passes home are part of the benefits that can be earned through the incentive program. There is no death penalty, the maximum sentence is thirty years.

We were allowed to speak to and question prisoners freely, no one was listening in or censoring our questions or the prisoners' responses. Overall, my impressions were positive. Even the prisoners agreed that they were treated well. A couple of the inmates were Contras and I honestly think they were just happy to be alive. Others who were awaiting trial pleaded their innocence to crimes they were accused of. I asked if they were allowed to criticize the government and they all answered no, not really. There are no legal impediments to criticizing the government but I was told that you could make enemies by doing it and that could be just as bad because they might then be accused of supporting the Contras.

None of the inmates complained about the conditions in the Chacara but a few complained about the courts and the fact that some had been held for over three months and were still awaiting trial. I do think that's really bad but even in our own country the court system can be slow and we have no excuse, we are a lot richer than this country and we're not in the middle of a war or facing an embargo.

I got the feeling that the prisoners were open with us, they seemed comfortable sharing their points of view without reservations. I don't know if all the prisons in Nicaragua are functioning at this level but this one is something to be proud of. It seems like there is a strong desire to rehabilitate, not simply to punish, another example of the hopeful nature of the Sandinista government.

Upon Reflection

I knew when I visited the prison that I was in the middle of a very controlled situation meant to promote a positive image of the Sandinista prison system. Despite my hopeful, pro-Sandinista bias, the nearly universal response that criticism of the government could be dangerous was of concern to me. I believe that a country's freedom can be gauged by the extent to which dissidents are allowed to speak their minds.

M.B.B 15

4/16/86, Wednesday

We had a charla with a representative of the FSLN who told us more stories of what it was like to live under Somoza. He also gave us some background on Carlos Fonseca, which I will recap here: Fonseca is considered the founder of the FSLN. His father was from a rich family and did not recognize Carlos as his son because Carlos was born out of wedlock. Carlos was raised by his mother, a poor washer woman, so class distinctions affected him from the moment he was born.

Carlos was in his early twenties when Fidel Castro and Che Guevara overthrew the Batista dictatorship in Cuba. He was inspired by that country's revolution because he saw many similarities between Cuba and Nicaragua, namely, minority ownership of the vast majority of the country's assets and resources; foreign intervention to prop up an unpopular government, political repression of dissenting views. He, along with two friends, created the Frente

Sandinista to fight against the Somoza regime. On November 8, 1976, Carlos Fonseca was shot and killed during a battle against Somoza's military guard but not before igniting a revolution in this country. The charla ended with the same words we've heard over and over again: the Sandinistas want freedom and peace but they want a peace that dignifies, not a peace that enslaves and they're willing to die fighting for it.

Escuela Nica at the march against the $100 million
in proposed aid for the Contras

When I got back home, some of the students from the school were waiting for me to help them create a banner for a big march protesting U.S. intervention taking place that afternoon. We made a banner reading, "The People of the United States join the struggle of Nicaragua", en español, of course. I outlined the letters and we all grabbed markers and colored them in. We held up our banner proudly and I was ready to leave it at that when Francie suggested we add "¡viva el internacionalismo proletario!" I have to confess that I hadn't really thought of myself as an internationalist until that moment, but I realized that what I've been doing with my expressions of solidarity and my support of the revolution are actions consistent with proletarian internationalism. How strange. I thought I was just supporting people who were trying to improve their way of life.

Upon Reflection

I don't think I truly understood the idea of proletarian internationalism while I was in Nicaragua. It wasn't until years later when I saw the power of multinational corporations that I came to understand that the working class must unite and work as a global entity in order to protect the rights and interests of workers around the world.

Carelia and friends at the march against the $100 million.

4/17/86, Thursday

Yesterday, the U.S. was expected to vote on the $100 million dollars that Ronald Reagan is trying to get in Contra aid. The money would be used to train and arm the counter-revolutionaries. Congress had voted against this before but Reagan is a man on a mission. The Sandinistas planned nationwide demonstrations with each town staging their own events. Esteli's march was comparatively small. The city of Leon put on a huge march, it was very impressive. It was in all the papers.

Even though it was a protest/peace march, the spirit was not somber or angry. People were having fun. It seemed like the whole town showed up carrying banners, flags, even handwritten signs scratched on notebook paper with repeated pencil marks. We chanted and sang songs and walked until our feet ached. In fact, Audrey and I decided to take a shortcut and sit at the park for a few minutes until the marchers came around again, then we quickly rejoined them, hoping no one noticed!

After walking to the school and back in the morning, then walking to the Salvadoran collective after lunch, and then participating in the march in the early evening, I was ready to put my feet up. Instead, Francie invited us to a party twenty-five blocks away. The party was another opportunity to notice how conversation is at the center of Nicaraguan social life. Even the younger people start talking and when they're fully engaged you can almost feel the connection between them. It seems that people here haven't lost the art of conversation; sometimes I think that there can be more intimacy in a good talk than in a good fuck. Didn't someone once say that the biggest sex organ is the human brain? I have to agree. Why am I thinking about sex so much lately? Oh yeah, because I'm not getting any.

I'm looking forward to going to Leon this weekend. I was hoping that Audrey and I could pool our money and hire a driver for the day but everyone is telling us that it's just as easy and much cheaper to hitchhike. Audrey wants us to take the bus but I don't want to spend three and a half hours on one of those overcrowded buses. They usually have people hanging out the doors and windows, and sometimes even riding on the roof hanging onto the luggage racks. There's a person whose job it is to squeeze people in. I can just imagine "ok, you move over there, you stand here, and you sit on the luggage rack and you can hang off the ladder." I don't want to do it. I've heard horrible things about bus rides in this country. Hitching is very common and a reasonable alternative. We see hitchhikers everyday. In fact, it's considered patriotic to share your ride because fuel is so scarce.

There's plenty of room on top!

4/18/86, Friday

Greetings from Leon. Audrey and I just got done with a giant cockroach hunt that proved unsuccessful. Now she's convinced that one of the flying, three-inch cockroaches has crawled between the mattress and the box spring in her bed. We went so far as to turn the mattress upside down, both of us screaming, squirming, and hopping from foot to foot as we flipped the mattress onto the floor. I had my jacket in one hand ready to swat the roach and Audrey had a notebook. We looked like two weird, primitive hunters wielding our makeshift weapons. The whole time we couldn't stop laughing because we felt ridiculous. In the end we couldn't find the cockroach, it magically disappeared. It's probably lying in wait until the lights go off. I'm just glad it's in her bed and not mine.

We hitched a ride here early this morning. We left Esteli at about 8:00 am and made it to Leon by noon. Frustratingly, we had to wait about forty-five minutes for the first ride until a whole bunch of us got picked up by Sandis and climbed atop an old army truck. That was a fun ride. We made friends with the other hitchhikers. One guy was coming to Leon and helped us get to the empalme, that is, he showed us the proper place to stand at the intersection with the road to Leon. There, we got a ride in under a minute on the flatbed of a huge rig that was carrying just a few pieces of machinery. There was plenty of room on the back. There were also several Sandinista soldiers aboard and some lively women telling jokes. I made friends with a cute Sandi named Jose or Paulino, or something like that, neither Audrey nor I caught his name. I just stared at his full, sexy lips as he talked. He looked to be in his mid-twenties, had smooth, olive skin and was long, lean and muscular. He looked good in his uniform and probably even better out of it. He told us he was stationed in Somoto which is not too far from Esteli. He also said he was studying English and asked me if I'd help him. Ha, of course I said yes and he said he would be heading

Lorraine Scognamillo, 2015

back this way next week and wanted to know if he could stop and see me in Esteli. Argh, he moves too slowly for me! Next week we might be dead. Audrey and I tried to convince him to come to Leon with us but he said he had to report back today.

Our third ride took only about two or three minutes to come along and drove us all the way to Leon. Hitchhiking was a great idea, it was fun talking to all those people. We checked in at the Hotel America which costs 2800 Cordobas per night, about three dollars. It's a pretty nice place, we have an indoor toilet and shower, there's even a ceiling fan in the room, luxurious by local standards. There are, however, one or more oversized cockroaches running around which are making us nervous. Audrey and I both hate bugs!

We decided to splurge on dinner at a restaurant called "Los Filetes," a very ritzy place where I had Chateaubriand for 4000 Cordobas, an exorbitantly expensive meal in Nicaragua but only about $4 in US currency. After that, Audrey and I went to a cool Cuban bar housed in a beautiful old world plantation-style mansion where the waiters wore stylish white guayaberas and some of the customers wore wide brimmed hats and smoked cigars. I was transported back in time. The heat made me crave a cold beer, but once again the curse of *"no hay"* struck so we had to make do with Cuba Libres. After that, we strolled back to the hotel. I hope the roaches don't get us tonight.

The Nicaraguan National Guard, Guardia Nacional, (aka Guardia) was a militia created during the occupation of that country by the United States from 1909 to 1933. In 1933, after the advent of the Good Neighbor policy and at the height of the Great Depression, the U.S. withdrew from Nicaragua and handed over control of the Guardia to Nicaraguan President Juan Batista Sacasa who in turn, appointed Anastasio Somoza Garcia as chief director of the Guard.

Somoza was educated in the United States and friendly to U.S. interests. With the strength of the U.S. Marine-trained troops under his control, Somoza quickly consolidated power. Between 1936 and his assassination in 1956, Anastasio Somoza Garcia ruled as dictator of that nation. He was supported by the Guardia which was largely funded by the United States throughout its existence.

For over four decades, the Somoza dynasty ruled Nicaragua, amassing wealth and land. When the Sandinistas overthrew the Somoza dynasty in 1979, many members of the National Guard fled into Honduras, where they regrouped and formed an counter-revolutionary force known simply as the Contras. As with their previous incarnation the Contras enjoyed generous, if at times clandestine, financial backing from the United States.

Church bombed by the Guardia in Leon

4/19/86, Saturday

Second day in Leon, Audrey and I went to the Cultural Center and later the Sutiaba Museum of Indigenous Anthropology which was about the size of my living room. Just goes to prove that size doesn't matter. They had lots of old artifacts and statues and they did a great job of telling the local history. After the museum, we walked around Leon, bought posicles, and sat in the park to people watch. We walked over to the old Guardia Nacional headquarters and then to see the church that the Somocistas bombed. It's crazy to imagine that Somoza would bomb his own people while they were attending mass, crazier still to think our government supported him! With our help, the Somoza dynasty plagued this poor country for decades.

One of my favorite American presidents is FDR so it made me sad to learn that he had once remarked of the late Anastacio Somoza Garcia: "Somoza may be a son of a bitch, but he's our son of a bitch." It seems like this attitude survived for decades and when Anastacio died, the U.S. continued to support his sons who subsequently became presidents of Nicaragua and would also make themselves useful to U.S. interests, while prospering at the expense of the Nicaraguan people.

Later, at the University we met the caretaker, a sun-beaten old codger with a friendly disposition. He liked us, so he took us on a little guided tour. He told us that the university used to be a seminary, then in 1812 it became the Real Universidad de la Inmaculada Concepción. It still looks like a church but the Sandinistas changed the name to the Universidad Nacional Autónoma de Nicaragua. The old man was obviously proud of the place. He told us that the City of Leon has been around since the early 1500s. "That's older than your country," he laughed. Yes, it is...pretty amazing.

Guardia Nacional Headquarters taken by the Sandinistas

We left the University and I remembered that I'd promised Nancy back in Esteli that I would take her watch that had been running slow in for repair if I could find a shop. We went back to the marketplace where a man had a stand with a little cardboard sign that read "Se arregla joyería y relojes" (jewelry and watch repair). He offered to fix Nancy's watch and said he could have it done in an hour while we shopped, so we walked around peeking in all the stalls.

I noticed a woman with several large, shallow baskets the size of truck tires spread out in front of her. Some had socks and underwear but the one that caught my eye contained a huge stash of birth control pills. I picked up one of the folding cartons and examined it. The pills were expired by nearly six months and had been sitting in the sun for who knows how long. I discreetly walked over to the shopkeeper and told her about the problem but she just smiled at me, saying "no, no, no," laughing at my ignorance while insisting they were still good. I walked away shaking my head, feeling sorry for the poor woman who had to rely on those pills for contraception.

Open air market

After about an hour, we went back to the watch repairman. He handed me the watch and we all looked at it until the minute hand twitched a couple of times. I paid him with the money Nancy had given me, but as soon as we left the market, the watch stopped again. We walked back to the stand and I had to argue to get Nancy's money back. In the end, he did fix the watch; it doesn't run slow anymore because now it doesn't run at all!

Sandino rests his foot on Uncle Sam

4/20/86, Sunday

Today is church day. We didn't actually attend any services but we did look at the buildings. Leon was colonized by Spaniards and there are lots of lovely old colonial buildings but the churches are the most ornate and beautiful. People flock to services on Sunday while outside, street vendors set up tables with colorful drapes, selling fruits, snacks and toys. We ate street food: repochetas, a sort of Nicaraguan quesadilla served with cabbage and cream. It's my new favorite dish, I ate until my stomach hurt.

We skipped dinner and went straight to Estudio 19, the local disco. It was hot and crowded and I wasn't really in a dancing mood. As I was standing there watching Audrey talk to an attractive middle aged man, I heard a voice next to me.

"Can I buy you a drink?" I turned around and a young man wearing glasses smiled at me.

"I already have a drink," I smiled at him weakly.

A single fist against agression

"But it's almost gone," he returned my smile.

Roberto is a medical intern, studying to become a doctor. He plans to move to the U.S., so he's been studying English and asked me if I would practice speaking English with him. His hair was neatly combed and he wore dark glasses that made him look bookish. I felt safe in his company, so I let him buy me another Cuba Libre and we chatted so he could practice his English. It was a stiff conversation because he had to think and construct sentences in his head before speaking and then he had to decipher every word I said before responding. After the second drink, we started speaking Spanish which was much more comfortable for both of us.

Roberto offered to give me a driving tour of Leon at night and I decided to take him up on it. I let Audrey know I would return shortly, but the city was pretty dark so it was an even shorter drive than I had anticipated.

We drove back and parked in front of the club.

"Thank you," I said. "You're the only person I've met in Nicaragua who owns a car. It was very nice of you to show me around."

"Do you own a car?" he asked.

"Yes."

"It's not so uncommon there, right?"

He wasn't expecting an answer, he was making a point. I wasn't sure if I was detecting irony or bitterness in his words.

"I'm more like you than you think," he continued. "We used to have cars, land and a nice house. We lost everything to the revolution."

Our eyes met. Now I knew it was bitterness.

"I bet this is a story you and your internationalist friends don't hear very often."

"You're right. Me and my internationalist friends are shown all the FSLN's successful projects. You don't like the Sandinistas very much, do you?"

He searched my face.

"I'm not accusing, I'm just asking."

"Somoza was corrupt, there's no doubt about it. Many people were happy to see him overthrown, but not everyone who fought against him is a communist. Now that the land and the factories belong to the people, the country is poorer than ever. The peasants can't produce like the old farm and factories could, so our rich lands are not profitable. Some peasants can't even fix a tractor if it breaks down, they don't have the money to buy the parts because they're still just working to stay alive. The factories that are still in business have very limited options to sell because of the embargo against the Sandinistas."

Revolutionary hero mural in Leon

He looked at me, waiting for a comment but I didn't have one. I knew that what he was saying was true. I thought of the sewing machines at the Salvadoran cooperative sitting idle because no one understood how to read the English language repair manuals. I had tried to help but my language skills did not include any knowledge of specific machine parts so my translations proved futile. Craft items for the store were being sewn by hand instead of machine.

"My brothers and sisters were all educated in the United States and I have family in Houston. My father was planning to send me to college there but our plans were changed for us since we made enemies with your government. Now I'm stuck here in Leon, but someday I hope to move there."

"This country needs doctors, too." The words came out of my mouth before I could stop them. I knew it wasn't what he wanted to hear.

"I will never get ahead here."

He touched my arm, which I took as a signal that I had to get out of there.

"Let's go back in," I suggested.

Once inside the noisy club, I felt like we were running out of things to say and I didn't want to go any further with him. He was trying to touch my arms and shoulders while giving me long, meaningful glances. I looked for an escape.

I smiled at a pretty looking boy who had a poofy bunch of curls falling over one eye. I think I used to have that haircut! He must have had ESP because he came over and introduced himself to me and Roberto, then he proceeded to talk only to me. Flavio was a war vet at 21, but he did not look like a soldier, I couldn't imagine it. About two minutes into our conversation, Flavio turned to me and asked if Madonna was pretty, which I found terribly funny for some reason. We both laughed, leaving Roberto perplexed.

I continued talking to both guys. About a half hour later, Flavio's friends showed up: a fair skinned guy named Rafa and a boyish looking young girl wearing black trousers, a white shirt and suspenders. She looked adorable. Flavio introduced her as Riquie (Enriqueta). The four of us hit it off. I think Robert felt a little excluded because he eventually excused himself and walked away.

The four of us hit the dance floor together and it was obvious, if only to the four of us, that Rafael was really dancing with Flavio and I with Riquie. I found Audrey and her friend on the dance floor and we all danced until they closed the place!

4/21/86, Monday

Audrey and I hitchhiked back from Leon this morning. We woke up early, despite staying up very late last night. We were out of the hotel by 8:00am and we caught a taxi to the outskirts of the city for a mil (about a dollar). We quickly caught a ride and made it back to Esteli before noon.

I have to go to the art collective this afternoon. I have a whole bunch of projects going. At first, I felt guilty switching from the farming and construction work but the school is happy, the collective is happy, and I'm much, much happier. In fact, it's really fun to be able to do something creative that helps people. The little seeds and plaques I've been painting have been selling and that makes me feel good because it means people like what I've made and the collective benefits from it.

Instead of hiding under the mosquito net, I think I'll be brave and go help Paca make lunch. She just got home and she's brought a sort of soft-looking cheese called coajada that one of neighbors made. Paca and the neighbors sometimes trade food because most people don't have refrigeration and leftovers can't be stored. When cooking a time-consuming dish, people often make enough to share with their neighbors and then trade food between households. There's no waste, food is bought in season and you have a great relationship with your neighbors - how smart!

Last week, Paca made beans and the neighbor made rice. Each household shared half of what they'd made, put the beans and rice together, and made a dish called Gallo Pinto. A loose translation would be something like Speckled Rooster, not because there's any rooster in it but because the colors of the beans and rice look like speckled feathers. I guess if you're creative and can't stand the thought of eating beans again, Gallo Pinto sounds more appealing.

4/22/86, Tuesday

I went to the school for a few hours this morning. I tried to hang back and not get in the way of the literacy teacher. As the students master the beginning levels of reading they are expected to help others. This strengthens their own learning and creates a feeling of camaraderie. It also takes the pressure off the teacher because the students become co-teachers.

One of the literacy classes I attended

I listened to a couple of young girls who wanted to read to me and then we discussed the reading. They enjoyed telling me about the history of their country and they brought it all to life by mixing in their personal anecdotes.

"You're lucky to be in Esteli. Almost everyone here fought in the revolution."

"And if you didn't fight, someone in your family did," her friend agreed. "Esteli played a big part in helping to overthrow Somoza."

They had stories of moms, dads, aunts and uncles joining the guerrillas or older siblings joining the literacy brigades.

When I went home for lunch, I talked to Carelia about my discussion with the young girls and she told me about her own days in the literacy brigade.

"We were, and still are fighting a war against ignorance," she explained. "All of Nicaragua is a classroom – there are people learning new things everywhere and people are expected to help without necessarily picking up a rifle."

After a training session, Carelia was sent out to the countryside to teach farmers and their families to read.

"It was hard for me at first, really hard, probably like it is for you coming here. Some places I went to didn't even have an outhouse or running water. We had to squat behind a tree and use leaves to wipe ourselves." I thought of how strange I had felt the first time I had to use newspaper instead of toilet paper. "It was difficult, but it gave us a chance to see how people live in the mountains and I'm glad I did it," Carelia said.

"They even sent brigadistas out to Bluefields on the Atlantic coast. That part of the country is very distant from the rest of Nicaragua.

Traditionally, they've been ignored by politicians. Do you know anything about Bluefields?"

"No, but I'd never heard of Esteli before I got here."

"The story goes that hundreds of years ago, a Portuguese ship filled with African slaves crashed on the eastern Atlantic shore. The slavers attempted to save some of their precious cargo, but the slaves overtook them and freed themselves, populating what is now Bluefields. The thing is, our cultures are very different and nobody has really tried to unify the Atlantic and Pacific coast as a nation. The government is hoping that by sending the brigadistas out to Bluefields there will be valuable cultural exchanges in addition to increased literacy."

"Is it working?"

Official Sandinista Literacy campaign goals

- *to eradicate illiteracy*
- *to encourage an integration and understanding between Nicaraguans of different classes and backgrounds*
- *to increase political awareness*
- *to nurture attitudes and skills related to creativity, production, co-operation, discipline, and analytical thinking*
- *to support national cohesion and consensus*
- *to strengthen the channels for economic and political participation*

"It's too soon to tell," Carelia said. Carelia told me that the brigadistas were encouraged to keep a diary during their time on the campaign to keep track of new experiences, new ideas, and questions that might arise. The diary was a learning tool for the volunteer teachers. Their learning was considered equally important to that of the literacy students.

Carelia and her friend on the street

4/23/86, Wednesday

This morning, I spent about two hours washing clothes. I was hanging my clothes on the line when Carelia came out to join me. She was sweeping the walk and asked me to save her my soapy rinse water so she could wash the walkway with it. She puts the radio on and the voices of Mexican singer Juan Gabriel and Spanish movie star Rocio Durcal immediately suck us in. The song is Dejame Vivir, and it's on heavy rotation. I've heard it everyday since I've been here. Suddenly Carelia is singing Rocio's part, asking her former lover to go away and leave her in peace. She walks over to me at the sink and gives me a pleading look as she sings in my face.

"No tenemos ya mas nada que decirnos solo adiós…"

I surprise her by belting out Juan Gabriel's part.

"No no no yo no me resignare, no, a perderte nunca…"

She cracks up and runs up the walkway, back to her broom.

I keep singing "aunque me castigues con este desprecio que sientes por mi…"

It's a real musical now, so I continue with the song, begging her not to throw our love away. She comes back in on cue.

"Para ti no tengo amor, no tengo amor ni tengo nada…"

On the second verse she comes at me with the broom.

"Déjame vivir, porque no me comprendes que tu y yo…"

"No tienes nada nada nada nada nada?"

"Que no, que no!"

We continue in this fashion going about our work as we sing. I hang the last of my clothes and hand her the bucket of leftover soapy rinse water. She makes like she's going to throw it at me and ends our little act with the lyric: "así es que déjame y vete ya!"

I duck into my room just as she splashes the soapy water on the walk, lathering it up with the broom. While singing duets is probably uncommon, singing aloud while doing chores is an everyday occurrence in this household. At least with Carelia and Lissette - they sing all the time, as loud as their lungs allow.

It's the same with the neighbors. You walk through the streets and hear singing coming from the open windows. Well, they're all open windows since few houses have glass panes. Their singing reminds me that art and music are about expression, not the impression you are going to make on others. Often, the singing is off key but it always makes me feel good to hear it, no matter what it sounds like.

This is the first time I've had a musical laundry session but even without the duet, washing clothes in Esteli is so different from washing in L.A.. Here, the tangible reward of clean clothes is directly linked to the physical labor of scrubbing them. At home, you put the clothes in a washing machine and go do something else and you never have to focus on the act of washing except to measure out the detergent and set the temperature. You are free to go do a job where you can make more money so you can buy machines or services that separate labor from reward. I've come to understand that money is not as powerful here because there are not as many things to buy and when something is available, it is sold cheaply enough so that anyone can afford it. There's less motivation to accumulate wealth. A lot of people share, trade and barter, making human relationships a kind of currency.

I'm not saying one way is better than the other, I'm not sure about that. It's just another big difference between how things are here and how they are back home. I'm sure that if I had to use the washboard every day of my life, I might be willing to sell my soul to the devil for a washing machine...or maybe not, the devil drives a hard bargain. Hmm, have I already made this deal?

Another thing that's strange is that I often think of myself as socially awkward but here, I like interacting with people, slowing down and getting to know them. At home I'm always on a mission. If I go to the market, I don't want to chat with the clerk, I want to pay for my groceries and get out but here I talk to everyone.

Upon Reflection

In case you're getting the wrong idea, you should know that I hate housework. I don't mind the process of doing it now and then but I hate that it feels like a Sisyphean task. Once complete, the satisfaction of accomplishing the job is very brief before it must be redone.

I've developed a bad habit of stopping for a fresco every time I pass the fresco shop. That's an average of four times a day, back and forth in the morning and back and forth after lunch. The nice thing is that you have to sit down and drink the fresco there because they don't pack them in baggies like posicles. So every Fresco turns into an opportunity to talk to someone. Everyone talks to everyone here. In fact, the fresco shop has turned out to be one of the best places to sit and interview people about the literacy campaign. I buy the fresco and they'll talk to me for an hour.

4/24/86, Thursday

We've started planning our despedida, which will consist of skits, music, and dancing. I've been asked to emcee and I'm also performing a song with three other students. It's called Carlos Fonseca.

I think all the students and families are emotional right now. This place has had an enormous impact on us and we know that we have our own revolution to create. We all want to take some of what we've learned here and share it with the people in the U.S.. We want Americans to know what's happening here, not just because it would help Nicaragua fulfill the goals of the revolution but because it would help Americans. We are such a big and powerful country that sometimes we forget that we could learn a lot from a tiny country like Nicaragua.

It's not just the literacy campaign that has created an impression on me. Although that is the reason I came here, I feel I've learned so much more. I know I'll be a better teacher because of this experience but I also think I'll be a better person. I wish I could help Gladys Baez do a speaking tour. My brief meeting with her has stayed with me. I grew up watching Mexican revolutionary movies that showed soldaderas and I wasn't ever really sure exactly what their roles were. Were they soldiers, or helpers, or what? Gladys is not only a combatiente, she's a commandante. She's calm, wise, articulate and very sure of herself. I understand now what Francie meant when she said that Gladys is very strong; to be a revolutionary leader it's not enough to be physically strong, you also need clarity and resolve. I discussed the idea of having Gladys do a speaking tour again with Francie and Mark and we were all concerned about her security. Maybe this is not the right time for her to be in the United States. Reagan has a lot of support right now.

I learned so much from Francie, too. Raising six daughters on her own, she's undoubtedly the head of the household and has a huge influence over the girls but she exercises her power in a very subtle way that makes her daughters feel guided and secure enough to make their own decisions. I've seen her give instruction once or twice; often it's a simple reminder. She's an amazing mother, but she is not defined by motherhood. She is defined by her struggle for justice and equality, by her ability to give herself completely to her beliefs.

My real mother fed me when I was hungry, nursed me when I was sick and loved me unconditionally. She gave me life and I will always love her. My Nicaraguan mother feeds my mind and nurtures my soul, and loves humanity, especially those who are oppressed. She has shown me how to live.

Upon Reflection

I can see now that the process of conscientization was already at work in me. These new revolutionary ideas were taking hold of me both consciously and subconsciously and initiated a change within me that aligned my actions to that ideology. I was experiencing transformative awareness, a consciousness with the power to create change.

I learned from all the girls. Even my little mouse, Adrianna, taught me the right way to tuck mosquito netting and the value of cow shit!

Francie just came by to give me a little going away gift she bought for me. It's a purse with "Nicaragua" stitched on it. She also sewed a rojo y negro scarf for me, the colors of the Sandinista flag. She tied it around my neck and called me *"compa."* It means *compañera*, companion or partner. We both started crying.

I really don't want to leave. Sure, I miss my loved ones and my music but a part of me really wants to stay here forever. It just seems that people here in Nicaragua are much more aware of what's really important in life. They're more concerned with humanity than with accumulating things or living in comfort, they strive for growth rather than material gain. The social and economic structures support this system of beliefs. People speak respectfully of a worker's deeds, a revolutionary's bravery, or a poet's ideas, not of the latest gadget someone purchased. Of course, there's not much to purchase. Instead of billboards inviting you to consume this or that new product there are billboards with revolutionary slogans, portraits of revolutionary heroes or a thought-provoking idea.

The things I once thought essential, I now understand to be trivial. So what if there's no toilet paper, there's self-determination!

4/25/86, Friday

We practiced our song all afternoon. It's a really cool song but it sure has a lot of words. In the end, we decided that each person would only sing one verse and then we'd all join in on the chorus and that worked out well. Everyone at the despedida knew the song and sang with us. It was powerful with everyone yelling "¡Presente!"

After our performances, our host parents shared stories about things they'd done with their "son" or "daughter" and everyone shared something they'd learned from the experience. It dawned on me that I had come to Nicaragua dreading the experience of having to live with strangers. I would have much preferred to stay in a hotel. I didn't realize that living with these families and coming to think of them as our parents, brothers, or sisters was a big part of what we had to learn. I was touched that my friends from the Salvadoran art collective showed up. They gave me a little painting of a Salvadoran landscape and several painted seed pendants they'd made for me, plus a bunch of FMLN pins and literature for me to take home and share with my friends.

Hold on. I hear some music outside my door.

Carelia and Lenin at home

Guess what? I was minding my own business, writing in my journal when Lenin, my little sister Carelia's boyfriend, brought me a serenata. He and one of his friends came by with a guitar and sat outside my door singing. I could see Carelia peeking from her room. It was really sweet and it would have been romantic if it had been an actual love interest serenading me instead of my little sister's boyfriend! But it was still a brand new experience for me. Truthfully, I can't imagine a guy back home doing anything like this. They sang all kinds of romantic songs for me and even a couple of upbeat ones at the end. My friend, Nancy, from the school came over about halfway through the serenade and sat on the doorstep with me and near the end Francie came out too. Carelia's great to conjure this up for me and Lenin is a sweetheart to go along with it. I bet I'm the only NICA student who got a serenade.

4/26/86, Saturday

I'm back at Hospedaje Norma. We must have gotten the worst room in the place but I'm too tired to care. I woke up at 5:30 this morning, I just couldn't sleep. Francie said she had to take a sleeping pill because she couldn't sleep either. This morning we all cried and hugged and kissed. I feel as though I'm being ripped in two. I really started to think of myself as part of this family. I love these people more than I would have ever thought possible. I miss them right now and I've only been away half a day. I guess it's knowing that I won't be seeing them for a long time that makes my heart ache. I intend to come back to Nicaragua as soon as I can.

When we got to Managua, a few of us went to the Robert Weimbus market for some shopping. Some people fly out tonight, others within the next few days. Many of the students want to take something back to a friend or family member. I didn't buy much, just a few postcards and some candy. Managua feels very different from Esteli, it doesn't have that neighborly feel that Esteli has and I found myself walking around the market wishing Lissette was with me to share the candy.

In the afternoon, I said goodbye to Nancy and Audrey. I'll miss them. Audrey in particular has been my best friend during this trip. She goes back to Boston and I don't know when I'll see her again.

More tears. To cheer ourselves up, a small group of us decided to go to a restaurant called Pizza Boom that some of the kids in this neighborhood said was really good. It wasn't. With pop music playing loudly over the speakers and colorful decor, I could see why kids would like it but they served the worst pizza I've ever had.

As we were sitting and not eating our pizza, the conversation went back to an incident that happened a few days ago. There had been a heinous suspected Contra attack in a place called Santa Cruz, just a few miles from Esteli. The reason I say that it was a "suspected" Contra incident is that despite the fact that everybody is pointing the finger at the Contras, I can't understand the logic of hacking up a little boy and an old lady with a machete. What could be the reason for that? How does it benefit anyone's cause? I don't like the Contras but it seems to me that people always want to blame every crime on them. I mean, the incident a few weeks back with the poisoning of the children in Condega is still being investigated, yet the rumor that the Contras poisoned the food is already being circulated. I wonder if some child killer is running around free and happy that the Contras are the prime suspects.

4/27/86, Sunday

This afternoon, a small group of the remaining NICA students and some of our newfound friends from the Norma went to La Yerba Buena, a sort of coffee house/bookstore. The books and political pamphlets are for sale but people seem to use this place as a library and printed material is scattered throughout. Yerba Buena sells coffee but the best drink here is the Yerba Buena, a cold mint drink with a healthy dose of rum. There was a poet reading when we first got here and when he was done, our group launched into a discussion of the situation in Libya, in reaction to a radio talk show we'd heard earlier in the day.

The U.S. bombed Libya a couple of weeks ago in retaliation for Libya's bombing of a German disco which Americans were known to frequent. Shortly after that, the Barricada published a copy of a letter that President Daniel Ortega sent to Muammar Gaddafi expressing his sympathy and support. I don't really know what to make of the whole thing. My impression of Gaddafi has been completely based on U.S. news reports. I've always seen him as hostile to Americans. I see Daniel Ortega as someone trying to defend his own country from intervention and I imagine Gaddafi sees himself the same way, but to go out of your way to attack Americans who are not in your country just seems like aggression.

Then again, just because Ronald Reagan says that Libyans are our enemies doesn't make it so. In fact, I don't trust our president at all. I don't really know if I'm getting the whole story here, anymore than I would if I were in the U.S.. I used to think that the press was impartial but time and time again I see that it isn't. It's not impartial in the U.S. and it certainly isn't in Nicaragua either. I'm not sure what to believe in anymore. When I was in Esteli, I could believe in the people. I saw how they behaved, how they aligned their actions to their revolutionary ideals, but big political machines anywhere are something altogether different.

The U.S. bombing of Tripoli was plastered over every front page and people here are still talking about it. I don't understand why Libya would bomb a place where there would be civilians in order to get at a few U.S. soldiers. It's criminal! It's just as horrible to bomb Gaddafi's residence and kill his baby daughter. I wouldn't support either action. I tend to think that both Gaddafi and Reagan are a little crazy.

How do you pick a side when both sides are wrong? What is a terrorist? I hear the word used so much and I'm getting really confused. I'm starting to think it's just a name to call your enemy when they attack you outside the battlefield, but then where is the battlefield? Is there an economic battlefield? I guess there is because that's what an embargo is. Also, the Contra war has a great deal to do with the economic problems of this country, since fifty percent of the national budget goes towards defense. I wonder if we are economically at war with other countries in a more covert way than I can imagine?

My father likes to say that all wars have to do with money. I hate to be cynical but I'm starting to think he may be right.

4/28/86, Monday

I'm so mad at Carrie right now. We managed to keep a safe distance from each other while we were in Esteli but here in Managua, we see a lot more of each other and she gets on my nerves. A group of us were riding in the back of a truck when I saw Carrie staring at me.

"What's up?" I asked her.

"You managed to keep your lipstick on and your legs shaved the whole time you were here," she said.

"And you managed to keep your legs hairy and your lips chapped," I said.

What followed was a little lecture about how makeup and shaving were tools to keep women oppressed. She sees herself as much more serious about the causes she embraces because she isn't concerned with her appearance. The thing is, she seems very concerned with what people think of her and other people's appearances. She had the audacity to make a crack about Francie wearing earrings with her olive drab uniform and I almost lost it. I moved within inches of her face and told her to shut up. People asked us to calm down and moved between us.

I remember having a conversation with Francie where she mentioned that I was much more like Nicaraguan women than like American women. I asked her why and she answered that it was not only because of my command of the language but because many of the American women at the school didn't shave their legs or groom themselves. I hadn't even noticed. All of Francie's daughters had pierced ears and they all wore earrings like I do. The older girls wear lipstick and shave their legs.

I think I understand where Carrie is coming from, I really do. I can see how people can become slaves to society's expectations, I think that happens in many ways. But I don't feel particularly oppressed by my appearance, in fact, I think that my appearance has often been a source of creative expression for me. Even as a kid I enjoyed dressing up, pretending to be a hula girl, or a mod in my plastic raincoat and matching boots. It's not the main focus of my existence but it is an undeniable part of me. I don't feel like I have to dress conservatively to satisfy convention but I also don't want to feel like I have to dress a certain way to defy convention. There are many ways to thwart oppression and succumbing to new oppressors is not the best way!

I remember the conversation I had with my little sister Paca about society's imposed standards of beauty. I can see why Francie wanted her to put up the working woman's photo along with the magazine model photos. We can't ignore the outside world, we have to look at the information and figure out what it means to us. Francie didn't want to force the girls to take down their pictures, instead she wanted them to have an example of a different kind of beauty for comparison. She doesn't want to indoctrinate, she wants the girls to think for themselves.

I don't care whether Carrie shaves her legs, I just want her to stop acting so superior and let the rest of us choose our own appearance.

4/29/86, Tuesday

Walking around Managua this morning, there is electricity in the air. Everyone is getting ready for the big May Day celebration. A few of the people that have been checking into the Norma have come specifically because they want to be in Managua for May Day. I'm so bummed that I'm going to miss it but I have to fly back home.

I spent some time in the early afternoon with a group of internationalists who were painting banners for tomorrow's festivities. Throughout the city, the hostels are full with people from all over the world. Black and red Sandinista flags are everywhere. I saw a woman on the street selling tee shirts with an image of Sandino in his large hat. I'm not a tee shirt fan but I bought one. I think I'll wear it home tomorrow. I managed to resist the impulse to act like a tourist until the last day.

In the evening we ended up back at the Yerba Buena where we were treated to an unexpected speech by a guy who claimed to be the P.L.O. (Palestinian Liberation Organization) Ambassador to Nicaragua. Does the P.L.O. even have an embassy? It was an interesting charla because the guy defied all my preconceived notions of what a member of the P.L.O. would be like and by that I mean he was not a madman. He was actually very reasonable. He told us about the plight of the Palestinian people and how many of them have lost their ancestral homeland through the creation of the Israeli state.

The speaker tried to disassociate himself and the P.L.O. from any terrorist activities, blaming it all on the Israeli secret police despite the fact that the P.L.O. has on several occasions, at least to the best of my knowledge, accepted responsibility for such actions. He was a persuasive speaker and seemed to be sincere, but I don't

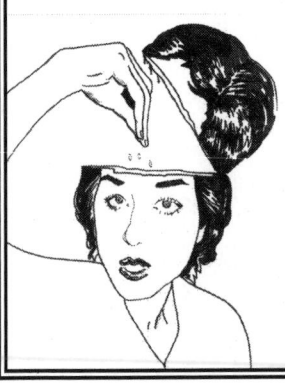

Seeds for Germination:

The Yerba Buena provided an opportunity for Dialogic, for dialogue between equals whose arguments could be evaluated based on reason and validity rather than acceptance of claims based on power or authority. I didn't realize that I had assumed my sources of information were unbiased. I had bestowed authority on the news media. I started to understand the importance of choosing various sources of information, being aware of who supports them and how they are funded.

know if I can believe what he said. It's just completely at odds with everything I thought I knew. In any case, I'm willing to at least listen to another side of the story.

It seems that quite a few people at the Yerba Buena (though not all) supported the Palestinian guy. He got a warm round of applause. Maybe I'm completely wrong about the P.L.O. You would think that as a person of Mexican heritage living in the United States I'd be able to relate to the idea that someone can take your land and then call you a foreigner. I do, of course but I'm also an American who sometimes benefits from my country's actions, whether I agree with them or not. My visits to Yerba Buena always seem to leave me feeling more confused than anything else. Maybe there's something in that drink! Oh yeah, there's a healthy dose of rum.

4/30/86, Wednesday

I've said all my goodbyes and I'm flying home today. I'm convinced that Nicaragua is a special place, different from any other place I've ever been. I can't quite put my finger on it, except that I can feel its heartbeat as though it was a living creature, a newborn baby eager to stand on its own two feet and take its place in the world.

The flight is already an hour late but it's on Nica time and so am I. I could live here... maybe. Better yet, maybe I can take a little bit of this spirit with me and infuse it into my own country. Looks like we're finally boarding.

Looking out the window, my eyes fill with tears when I think of what I'm leaving behind. I've fallen in love with Nicaragua, with its people, their ideas, their tenacity. How did they do it? How did they manage to become so strong and so determined as to overthrow the oligarchies and to continue to fight for autonomy despite pressure from a country as rich and powerful as the United States?

They're an inspiration. El Amanecer del Pueblo, the title of the literacy textbook means "the dawn or awakening of a people." How appropriate. I wonder, once you've been awakened, can you ever go back to sleep? I wouldn't think so, but then, why isn't this feeling of self determination more common when there have been revolutions all over the world throughout history? Do people fall back asleep, lulled by complacency?

We're being told we have to get off the plane in San Salvador. I thought we'd stay on the plane and fly directly to Houston but that's not the case.

I'm in the air again, we just took off from a stop in San Salvador where we had to get off and go through customs before continuing on to Houston. Waiting in San Salvador airport, my stomach gave a little twist when a fully armed Salvadoran soldier walked by me.

I'm wearing a tee shirt with the image of Augusto Sandino and my carry-on bag is full of FMLN plaques, buttons, and pendants made by me and others at the Salvadoran art collective in Esteli. Basically, I was a walking billboard for the overthrow of the Salvadoran government. Maybe I'm just being paranoid but I heard so many horror stories from the Salvadoran refugees who I worked with at the collective and on the farm about the ruthless police and military tactics used against anyone who questions the government that I felt pretty scared. Anyway, I'm glad we're in the air now. I'm feeling a little bit queasy. I don't understand why, I hardly ate anything this morning except for sugary lemonade, a piece of pastry, some orange juice, and a couple of cookies...maybe I did eat the wrong thing.

I hope Bruce remembers to pick me up in L.A.. I wonder how I'll feel about being back in the U.S.. It's like traveling from one world to another. Even though I've been living there for most of my life, I have a feeling it will all seem different to me now. I'm sure my thinking has changed. I've changed.

I keep thinking about how people would sometimes mistake me for Nicaraguan. I felt Nicaraguan. I dressed, ate, lived, breathed, dreamed and even began to talk Nicaraguan. Some people said I had a Mexican accent and kidded me about it but for the most part I was treated like a "*compa*." I still remember the first time Francie called me a *compa* - a *compañera*, a companion in struggle. Shortly after that, other people started to call me *compa* and I felt so happy to be included, to be able to share their revolution. The word was like a tiny pipe bomb in my soul, shattering my deluded and sheltered view of the world.

There is a Nica saying: "*Entre Los Pueblos, No Hay Fronteras*": Between people, there are no borders. I've met so many people here from all over the world who are volunteers, writers, activists, people from all walks of life who want to help and see self-determination succeed. Some may see themselves as proletariat internationalists but others are just idealists who think that success here means success in other places is possible.

I don't think we could have this kind of revolutionary change in the United States, at least not now. I remember reading Brave New World many years ago in school and thinking that Soma comes in so many forms. Most of us in the U.S. have our basic needs met. Food, shelter, and TV are the Soma of the working class. We have just enough to keep us in a complacent stupor. We're missing enough discomfort to provoke change.

We're landing in Belize, so I've gotta take a break. I wish I had some film so I could take a picture of this tiny Belize airport!

Back in business. They handed out mani a little while ago, which looks a bit like a peanut but they're so hard, it's like no peanut I've ever eaten. Nothing's quite the same in Central America. I'm giving up on these before I break a tooth. I'm still queasy anyway. It's ironic that when I was in Nica I never felt sick to my stomach despite all the homemade food I was eating and now that I'm on the plane eating "healthy," hygienically packaged food I feel a little ill. Maybe it's just that my system was used to running on beans, tortillas, coffee, and lots and lots of sugar! I did find out that sugar is rationed but you're allowed approximately two pounds of sugar per person per week. Jesus, what kind of diet would they have if it wasn't rationed? Here's a bit of trivia: toilet paper is rationed at 2 rolls per family per month. Beer is considered a luxury but ron is the people's drink. No wonder we drank it so often. I'm going to miss Flor de Caña, I hope I can find it in the U.S..

I'm a little worried by all these stops. The fact that the initial flight out of Managua was late will delay our arrival into Houston. I don't want to miss my connecting flight to Los Angeles or end up sleeping in the airport! I inadvertently passed through an x-ray machine carrying my purse back in Managua. All my exposed film was in the purse. I hope the film isn't damaged. It would be so sad if all my pictures were ruined. I want to be able to share this experience and it will all be easier to remember with the photos and the diary. Although, I can't imagine forgetting any of it. Esteli has left a mark on me.

I'm going to try to take a nap and I'll write again later.

I'm on my way to L.A. now. I barely made my flight! We got into Houston late and I had to go through customs before catching the connecting flight. The lines were enormous. When I walked up to the immigration officer, he asked me if I had been on a farm and I had to say yes. He sent me into a different section where a more thorough investigation of my farm visitation could be discussed. The section was coded red and in my mind that meant stop. I was cursing inwardly for not lying about where I'd been but they walked me over to the red section and I noticed that the non-restricted green section, where everyone else was being sent, was super congested while the red section was just me. I walked over to the inspection area and the customs officer smiled at me. He wasn't stressed because nobody was in his line. I smiled back, instantly at ease.

"So you were on a farm?" he asked.

"Yes."

"What did you do on the farm?"

"Plant tomatoes."

"Is that all?"

I thought for a minute. "Sweat."

He laughed, opened my suitcase, picked up a blouse, tossed it back in and told me to have a nice day.

"I'll do that if I manage to catch my flight!" I said, remembering that missing it was a distinct possibility.

"Which flight are you supposed to catch?" the customs officer asked, flagging someone from the airport to come over and help me. The woman quickly checked on my flight.

"You're about to miss it!" she said, genuinely concerned. She flagged a cart over and asked the driver to rush me to the boarding gate. "I'll let them know you're on your way."

The flight attendant was literally holding the door for me. She looked annoyed. "Hurry, hurry, you're holding up the flight!"

I ran in, shoved my stuff in the overhead and buckled up. Next stop, L.A..

5/1/86, Thursday

It's hard to get out of the habit of writing this journal. The drive home last night was like a hallucination, it all felt surreal. There were bright neon lights everywhere announcing bail bonds, fast food, pawn shops, hotels, liquor stores. I couldn't believe how many lights there were. I couldn't even see the sky. It felt like a dark tent illuminated by artificial lights, no stars.

Inside, the car was cold. Bruce picked me up but I can tell that it's over for us. We hugged and kissed and it was friendly enough but when I tried to tell him about my trip he seemed to be somewhere else. We had seven good years but now we seem to have completely different interests. I hoped our time apart would allow us the space to sort things out and maybe make a go of it again but our time apart has just made me realize that we are pulling in different directions. It's sad and I know it will be hard because he was my best friend for so long but I don't feel like crying about it right now.

I don't know if I'm tired, jet lagged, or just suffering from culture shock, possibly it's a combination of all three but I'm feeling out of sorts. Can a person have culture shock returning to her own country? It's weird, I was born here and right now this place feels foreign to me. Things that were once familiar and hardly noticed now stand out in contrast with my recent experiences. There were no roosters and chickens to wake me up this morning, I set my alarm clock instead but I didn't need it because my inner alarm clock woke me up at the right time. I got in my car and drove to the market to buy a box of cereal and a carton of milk. I didn't talk to anyone or say hello to anyone along the way. There was no singing coming from the open windows of neighbor's houses. I didn't feel the cobblestones beneath my feet as I walked to my destination; instead, I was in a vacuum, in my own little capsule with a radio piping in recorded music. At the market, bright overhead lamps illuminated the abundant, perfectly shiny produce. Shelf after shelf of packaged foods filled the aisles of a building four times the size of a market in Esteli. One aisle, devoted entirely to different varieties of paper included scented and unscented toilet paper in single, medium, or large packs with flowers printed on them, textured, or plain. We have so much but we're also missing so much.

I left the market with much more than I came for. That's how it works here. I'll put stuff in the cupboards and fridge and hopefully I'll eat it, but half the time my fresh fruits and vegetables rot. It's strange, in Nicaragua my family and most of our neighbors did not have a refrigerator and it forced us to eat fresh food in season and to share and cooperate with our neighbors. Here, we don't have to do that. We are free to isolate ourselves, free to waste. It makes me wonder if we own our conveniences or if they own us. I've always sort of felt like a loner anyway so maybe this works best for me and yet it felt good to share and cooperate.

Truthfully, I'm confused. I eat a bowl of cereal while watching TV, something I've done nearly my whole life, and I'm unable to focus on the program. There is a part of me that wants to stay in the present. There is a part of me that does not want to escape into the fantasy on the television. There is a part of me that affirms that I don't need the simulation of life that TV and movies provide. In Nicaragua, people were living in the present, fully engaged in whatever they were doing at the time they were doing it. I already miss that. Some people might pity them: poor things - they have no TV, but having no TV means they can ignore the simulation and focus on real life.

5/1/86, Thursday PM

I'm ready for bed. Work was uneventful. I got my classroom set up and my lesson plans are all done. There was a little cloud of melancholy that hung over my head all day. I guess part of it was knowing that it was May Day and that back in Nicaragua everybody would be celebrating their revolution, their freedom, their autonomy. Here, it's just another work day, except for me - because inside of me there's a revolution, there's a permanent change that won't let me fall back into the stupor. I'm awake.

Epilogue

My revolution happened from the inside out over a prolonged period of time. It started with my visit to Nicaragua and continues every day of my life. There's always a news story, a personal interaction, or a provocative idea that requires me to face the world as a teacher/student, that requires me to step outside my comfort zone and engage in praxis.

As I was editing this journal, I started thinking about how much time has passed between now and when it was written. The places and people I describe have all changed but the lessons I learned taught me what it means to be strong, showed me the limitations of wealth, the value of dialogue, and the importance of fostering and developing critical consciousness. Those lessons feel timeless.

While I was in Nicaragua, I questioned my ability to make the huge changes I knew needed to be made. I wanted to stop President Reagan from funding the Contras. I wanted to bring Comandante Gladys Baez to the United States so she could inspire others. I wanted to change our educational system so that it focused on critical thinking rather than simply depositing facts. All those things seemed like they were beyond my control. I suppose that it might have made sense to go back to my old ways and accept defeat, but I couldn't. I had seen David take on Goliath and I started looking for my own slingshot.

As soon as I got back, I started making changes in my teaching style to include more dialogue and I structured my reading classes so that they went from concrete to abstract. That was a short lived party because training children for taking tests became a priority of my employers and made it difficult for me to provide the type of education that did more than create receptacles for filling. I didn't want to program students, I wanted to help them think for themselves.

I've come to understand that before policy changes can take place, the population's understanding of education has to change, values have to change. My opportunity to change the world begins with me and extends as far as the ideas I manage to share with others. I hope my spark of revolution can ignite the process of critical consciousness in you. I hope that as you read my diary, you questioned your own beliefs, mine, and any beliefs which have been deposited into you through the banking method.

I leave you with a final thought: the revolution starts within.

Acknowledgements

I'd like to be able to call this book a self-published endeavor but the truth is that it was a joint project. I had a lot of help.

I would not want anyone to have to work their way through my misspellings, typos, and lack of (or excessive use of) commas. Ditto for the endless rambling and mental meandering that are my signature traits. Luckily, I'm not going to babble, babble on this time, thanks to the tireless efforts of Greg, Madison and Sophia Velasquez. If my voice comes through in the writing and you understand my motives, it's due to the tough-love literary criticism of Tummy Ache's Raquel Gutierrez and Valentina Silva.

Besos to Rudy Bleu for being my self-publishing mentor and for putting me in touch with Blake Besharian. Blake, thank you for not killing me every time I changed something and for drinking my microwaved ginger tea and pretending you liked it. Your guidance has been invaluable.

I've said it before and I'll say it again: I am a love tycoon. When they found out I didn't have all the images I wanted to illustrate the book, my friends Kelly Thompson and Lorraine Scognamillo came to the rescue, making original artwork for a couple of the entries. They said they would have done it even if I hadn't gotten them drunk.

I want to profess my love for Cristy C. Road, who came up with the front and back cover for this book in two weeks! I am her fan and am thrilled that we can share this creative endeavor.

Finally, to all the people who read and supported Violence Girl, you are the reason I decided to write another book. You gave me courage. Your emails, letters, positive reviews, invitations to classrooms, bookstores, and record stores were an affirmation that my voice was being heard. You told me about your lives and pointed out things we had in common. You made me feel like we were companions on a journey. This book is for you.

About the Author

Alice Bag was the lead singer of the Bags, a 1977 punk band that was at the forefront of the early west coast punk scene. Her performances were documented in the film The Decline of Western Civilization. Alice has been involved in numerous musical projects, most of which have included other female musicians and artists.

In 2011, Alice penned her first book, Violence Girl, From East LA Rage to Hollywood Stage - A Chicana Punk Story. Violence Girl chronicles the story of Alice's upbringing in East L.A. and her eventual migration to Hollywood to help usher in the first punk wave.

Alice is a blogger, turned author and a former bilingual elementary school teacher. She is an outspoken activist and feminist. Her hobbies include painting, baking and causing trouble.

Made in the USA
San Bernardino, CA
14 March 2020